PRAISE FOR *Living AWAKE*

"*Living AWAKE* is a treasure chest of insight, wisdom, and practice. This forty-day journey invites the reader to know herself with love, and to then lavish that love on others. In a day and age when a lot of spiritual pabulum is in the marketplace, Mary Bea Sullivan serves up real food for body, mind and spirit, food that is like the bread of communion, giving bread so that the reader can offer bread."

—Rev. Mary C. Earle, *Days of Grace: Meditations and Practices for Living with Illness*

"Mary Bea Sullivan's *Living AWAKE* is a wonderful manual for the spiritual seeker who thinks globally and is not afraid to move beyond the confines of his or her belief system. Using a combination of personal narrative and insights into the sacred traditions of the world's religions, Mary Bea offers practical exercises for everyday people whose hearts ache for 'something more.' She writes as a seasoned mentor well familiar with the territory, inviting the uninitiated to take the first steps toward 'living awake' because it is a journey she herself has taken. The forty-day format involves a minimal time commitment but provides both continuity and depth, allowing the pilgrim to progress at a comfortable pace, secure under her tutelage. A must-read for spiritual guides and spiritual seekers who will undoubtedly look for a sequel!"

—Elizabeth-Anne Stewart, PhD, *Jesus the Holy Fool*

"There is a deep hunger today to have a more intimate experience with the Divine. *Living AWAKE* is a great way to get started or to get back on your journey with the Divine. This meditative guide comes from the deep wisdom of both eastern and western spirituality, yet it is simple and short enough that it can realistically be done in the midst of our busy lives. And if you stick with it for forty days, you will have established a habit that becomes natural to you and you will be living more awake."

—Rev. Bob Haden, Director of the Haden Institute

FEEDBACK FROM
Living AWAKE PILOT GROUPS

"Finding a few minutes each morning to reflect on being a more loving, grateful, forgiving person has influenced each day tremendously."

—Kelly Ross-Davis, Education Director, HIV Clinic

"I'm really thrilled to have this in my life right now. It is just what I was looking for (or not looking for!). I am going through changes now that need prayer and discernment; this has brought me back to some accountability and focus. I love feeding my soul!"

—Debi Swaney, Business Owner

"I read *Living AWAKE* when I was deeply involved in caring for a dying parent. It offered me wonderfully fresh and creative exercises to help me savor life, appreciate my blessings, and reclaim moments when I felt most alive. I looked forward to Mary Sullivan's wisdom every morning to brighten my day."

—Jeanne Jackson, College Administrator

"I am so loving this! I have a sacred space and have taken quiet time with my Higher Power daily for over twenty years. I am amazed at how these activities are raising my awareness in so many areas!"

—Ann Caretti, Wellness Consultant

"This is powerful. I am struck by the 'letting go' theme, and it's been a great reminder to me to release the things I need to let go in my own life."

—Katy Smith, Chaplain and Episcopal Deacon

"I LOVE the stories! Just reading them has helped."

—Diane E. David, Program Integrator for the U.S. Department of Defense

"I have loved every entry and have loved being a part of this!"

—Kathy Thomson, Attorney

Living AWAKE!

forty days toward renewal

To Brantley —
Blessings on your journey!
MayBS

Mary Bea Sullivan

Living AWAKE: Forty Days Toward Renewal

Published by Wheatmark®
610 East Delano Street, Suite 104, Tucson, Arizona 85705 U.S.A.
www.wheatmark.com

ISBN: 978-1-60494-523-2
LCCN: 2010937290

Back cover photo of Mary Bea Sullivan by Theresa Burns

Also by Mary Bea Sullivan

Dancing Naked Under the Moon
Uncovering the Wisdom Within

To my parents,

Margaret Mary and Dave Krohn.

Thank you for instilling in me
at an early age
the belief
that we are all connected
to something GREATER
than ourselves.

Contents

Contents

FOREWORD

WHAT HAPPENS WHEN THE STORY we've been telling ourselves about ourselves becomes too painful? What happens when we wake up and find that the known and familiar world we thought we knew is no longer there? There are treasures available to us to help us see the world anew and make a fresh start. Mary Bea Sullivan is a wise guide because she—through her own experience —knows that being and becoming human is a craft that requires practice, like playing a musical instrument or learning how to paint. Here the reader will find a series of practices over a classic period of forty days that will heal the soul, refresh the mind and heart, and open up new pathways. One of the great joys of being connected to the great spiritual practices and traditions available to us is to discover that there are stories all around us which help us look differently on the little psychodramas going on inside us, like some old movie or TV show. These daily practices will help the reader get out of places where he or she has gotten stuck. What a relief to know that there are stories out there other than our own—stories that help us live from a deeper and lovelier place, practices which open us up to the new, ways of reaching out which will bring us joy, glory, and surprise!

—Rev. Alan Jones, Dean Emeritus of Grace Cathedral
and Honorary Canon of Chartres Cathedral
San Francisco, CA
September 2010

INTRODUCTION

WHAT IN YOUR HEART IS aching? What in your soul is stirring? Can you give yourself the gift of fifteen minutes a day? With yourself? With the Divine? Can you trust that in showing up each day you will find renewal? I'll answer for you. Yes! I know you can and will because I did.

Preparing to take my children, Brendan and Kiki, to college gave me the impetus to birth this book. Somewhere between weekend orientation excursions and shopping for bedding, mini-refrigerators, and underwear, I made a commitment to write a reflection and an accompanying spiritual practice each day—for forty days. I felt compelled to write and share, inviting those who follow my blog to join me in the reflections and practices.

You might be wondering why I would take on a new project during such a stressful time. Writing has always been a healing way for me to find clarity. And this was a difficult time, filled with unexpected and unwanted waves of sadness over both kids leaving home at once; and it was a fertile time, full of bursts of energy and ideas. During those forty days, writing and following the simple spiritual practices I created soothed me.

Why forty days? Research shows it takes a good twenty-one days to develop a new habit. I wanted that much time and then some. I also hoped for a period of time with spiritual significance. The number forty repeatedly cropped up.

I thought about Noah in the ark for forty days. Jesus fasted for forty days and forty nights in the desert after his baptism. When I researched the number forty, I found that every mention of forty days or forty years in the Bible signaled a time of testing that led to renewal and the fulfillment of promises. I found a quote by the Sufi Master Shah Nazar Ali Kianfar: "Forty days...is the mystical number of the course of perfection, a course that leads to an experience of the true essence of one's humanity." My research and my heart convinced me; I would write something every day for forty days.

Getting to the writing was often hard. The day my husband, Malcolm, and I took Kiki to college, just two weeks after dropping off Brendan, I simply wanted to curl up in a ball and cry. Writing about dropping my children off at college allowed me to see that my empty, kid-free hands were also open to receiving and giving thanks. I wrote about reclaiming pieces of myself and was inspired to go mountain biking again for the first time in decades. As I approached life with an eye toward observation, I found that all of my senses, my very soul, re-awakened.

I was heartened and honored by emails and phone calls from my readers, who were taking a few minutes each day for the reflections and practices. They shared with me their expressions of joy and of "living from a deeper place." Learning that others were benefiting as well, I was motivated to share the material further—to invite you to join us.

Thanks for coming along. Let's approach this in the spirit of playful exploration and head out on the trek together.

Before we begin, I'll tell you a bit about me, your guide on this adventure. Early on, most of my symbolism and experience of God was framed by being raised in a large, Roman Catholic family. I left the Catholic Church in my twenties because women were not allowed to become priests. Still, I have an appreciation for the tradition and am grateful for having grown up with a sense of connection to something greater than myself.

Over the years, I have studied various faith traditions, most notably Tibetan Buddhism. I have had the privilege of briefly studying with Lama Norlha Rinpoche from the Kagyu lineage. It was Lama Norlha who encouraged me to return "home" to Christianity and follow that path deeply. Eventually I landed in the Episcopal Church. Frequently, it is in the natural world where I most deeply experience the Sacred.

It is my belief that we honor and respect the Creator by treating all human beings with honor and respect. The more I learn about and understand other traditions, the deeper my own faith becomes. I need not be threatened by another's practices or try to "win them over" to my side. I believe I am simply called to love as Christ loved.

Ten years ago after the death of my dear friend, Rhonda Holman, I started an end-of-life care non-profit, Project Compassion, in her memory. My first book, *Dancing Naked Under the Moon Uncovering the Wisdom Within* explores my painful spiritual journey after Rhonda's death.

Losing Rhonda and then leaving a sixteen-year marriage profoundly changed my life. In order to find meaning from the losses, I chose to dedicate my life to creating opportunities for people to live as fully as possible in our fleeting world. This has allowed me to follow my passion. I lead spiritual retreats, workshops, and wisdom circles. I write about spiritual awakening and serve one-on-one as a spiritual companion. As I have already mentioned, I am the mother of two college-age children. Being their mom is one of my greatest joys. I live on a beautiful, deep lake in Alabama with my husband, Malcolm. It is a second chance for love for both of us. Malcolm is a fun and gentle soul who has been minister and chaplain to many for over thirty years. I am grateful for his willingness to seek and grow with me.

Setting out on this forty-day journey was a reminder for me to live as fully as possible. What did I learn? Many things: that showing up truly is half the battle; that I can be, unfortunately, very good at wasting time. Yet, if I am truly committed and organized, I can carve out time for something as crucial as recharging my spiritual battery. I learned that excuses debilitate, dedication empowers. Perhaps most importantly, I gained a renewed appreciation for the gift of the journey. This forty-day experiment indeed was a time of renewal for me and fulfillment of promises unspoken. Looking back, it was as if I blew away dust that had been covering a hidden spark within.

I wish all of this for you as well. I invite you to walk with me these forty days, to create space and explore the questions crying out from within. My deepest desire for you is that by taking just a few minutes each day you will strengthen the connection between your heart and your soul, igniting a spark from within. I hope that you too will find unimagined gifts. I trust that as you explore and expand your own experience of the Sacred, you will be a light for others along the path.

Introduction

WHAT TO EXPECT

Each day you will be given a reflection to read and a corresponding spiritual exercise, such as a prayer practice, a journaling prompt, or a simple mindful activity. A natural progression through the days and weeks reinforces and deepens your experience as you go along. I encourage you to commit to a minimum of fifteen minutes each day; some days you may wish to spend more time. In honor of simplicity, I have refined the reflections and exercises, stripping away excess. Life is complicated enough—one daily reflection and one practice will suffice.

You may find that reading the reflection is all you can manage some days. Fine. You will still benefit from taking even that small amount of time to absorb the day's message. It will stay with you.

When you finish the forty days, you might want to start over again or go back and re-experience your favorite days. Listen to the spirit within you and trust you will know what serves your highest good.

IS THIS ONLY FOR CHRISTIANS?

No. Many of the exercises are rooted in the Christian tradition, but all can be modified for people from different traditions or those who claim no tradition. In each of the exercises it is my intention to tap into the Eternal Source toward which all traditions point. I encourage you to keep an open mind. I believe that faith expands and deepens by experiencing different approaches to the sacred.

SABBATH DAYS...DAYS 7,14, 21, 28, AND 35

The instructions on days 7, 14, 21, 28, and 35 invite you to spend an extended period of time with your practice. This is optional. Feel free to be creative and switch around when you do the Sabbath exercises to accommodate your needs. Remember, these extended forms of retreat are a reminder that even God took one day off a week.

Introduction

Words can be "triggers." Many of us experience "God" as a benevolent presence in our lives; for others "God" has been used in harmful ways. Some of us read words like "Spirit," "Sacred," and "Divine" and feel spacious connections; others are turned off by their non-traditional feel. If a word creates a stumbling block along the way, feel free to replace it with one that works better for you. Make the material your own. Consider opening your heart to new language for expressing what is sacred.

WHAT WILL I NEED?

First and foremost, you will need a desire to deepen your connection to LIFE: to yourself, to the Sacred, to the world around you. You will be given opportunities to journal, make notes, record the yearnings of your soul. Perhaps you would like to treat yourself to a beautiful new notebook or journal and pen. A simple pad of paper will do as well. I will encourage you to enjoy nature. A comfortable pair of sneakers will be handy for those days.

You may want to ask a friend or family member to walk this journey with you—as a Living AWAKE Buddy. Or you may want to bring together a small group to meet each week to share experiences as a Living AWAKE Circle. There are instructions for creating and facilitating Living AWAKE Circles at www.marybeasullivan.com.

Smile, Breathe, and Welcome to Living AWAKE. I invite you to use these forty days to open up to seeing yourself and your life in new ways. I hope you will cloak yourself in a spirit of exploration and wonder. I am excited to take this walk with you.

Thanks for joining me!

Mary Bea Sullivan
September 2010

DAY 1

Sacred Space

Your sacred space is where you can find yourself again and again.
Joseph Campbell

SPACE MATTERS. IN THE 1970s, women demanded more life-giving environments in which to give birth. Hospitals responded by creating birthing rooms with softer lighting and more comfortable furniture. For the first time, women were able to stay in the same room for labor, delivery, and recovery. In explaining why she plans to train as a midwife, Harvard Divinity School student Cemelli de Azlan notes, "the birthing room is the place where we open our eyes for the first time and invite the light."

How might you claim time and space to "invite the light"?

Years ago I began an almost-daily meditation practice. At first, finding time to "sit" was nearly impossible, my resistance great. Over time, showing up became more natural. Eventually, I craved a sacred space that I could return to time and again. After scouting around the house, I chose a cedar chest I had lined with washi paper as my "altar" and placed it in my bedroom. Each day after taking the children to kindergarten, I would return to this spot in my bedroom, light a candle, sit cross-legged on the floor with a pile of pillows, and meditate for fifteen or twenty minutes. *Let the work and laundry pile up*, I told myself. *I need this.*

I have moved many times since then and in every new home have taken pleasure in creating a place where I can reconnect with the Divine, myself, and with practices that remind me to simply BE.

I observe my sacred space now, as I write. In this home my space is an old chest placed underneath the window that overlooks our perennial garden. On top of the chest sit beautiful cards, gifts from people whom I love, and other meaningful items. This is my altar.

In front of the altar is a purple meditation cushion, a birthday gift from Malcolm. Some mornings I approach the cushion as a lover eager to return to the arms of her beloved. Other days, washing the dishes seems more appealing than entering that purple prison. But it is there, always, waiting for me, ready to receive me. All I need to do is show up, take a deep breath, and be present.

Sacred space could be as simple as a corner of a room with a chair or an entire room. Rev. Mary Earle tells the story of a young mother who told her children, "When I am sitting on the third step, you are not to disturb me." That was her sacred space.

Another woman, a frequent traveler, found a beautiful rock on a trip to the sea that reminded her of the Sacred. She claims this rock as her sacred space and packs it with her wherever she goes. She says, "As soon as I place it in my hand, and feel the rock's cool smoothness against my skin, I begin to settle into silence."

Practice

Setting up a Sacred Space

Take a few moments of quiet time. Consider possible areas and choose an inviting place you'd enjoy visiting regularly, a spot where you could invite the Sacred to join you.

How would you like to create beauty in your space? Walk around and collect objects that hold special meaning for you. Perhaps you'll choose flowers from the garden or a drawing from a child. Place what you've gathered in an appealing way in your space.

Sit for five minutes today to get started.

If you already have a daily ritual and/or sacred space, might you benefit from "refreshing" it in some way? New candles? A new prayer? Perhaps it is lovely as it is; if so, give thanks. Over time, let your space evolve and change as you do.

DAY 2

Taking Stock

An unexamined life is not worth living.

Socrates

In *Co-Active Coaching*, Laura Whitworth uses an effective coaching tool called "The Wheel of Life." Using the wheel, clients rate their satisfaction with various aspects of their lives such as Health, Money, Family/Friends, Career, etc. Having administered this assessment many times, I believe we are often unaware of dissatisfaction within even the most important parts of our lives.

One of the categories on the "wheel" is Fun/Recreation. Upon completing her "wheel," one of my clients looked at me astounded, "I never even think about having fun. I can't believe that it never enters my mind. I think about getting my work done, cooking, cleaning, taking the kids to their sports, anything except fun!" After this revelation she began hiking in the woods with friends a couple of times a week. Making this one change not only increased her sense of happiness; she also felt soothed by being in nature, supported by the other women, and healthier from the exercise.

What if we add "spiritual life" to our wheel of life? You have made a promise to yourself for these forty days. Something within you was drawn to this idea. Perhaps it would prove beneficial to take a few moments to identify some of your hopes and dreams for this time; "take stock" of how life is for you at this moment.

PRACTICE

Taking Spiritual Stock

Bring your journal with you to your sacred space. Sit for a few minutes in silence. SMILE. Agree to play with this idea of taking stock of your life. Answer the following questions, taking a few minutes with each one. If you really start rolling on one question—let it rip. You can always come back to the others when you have more time. Say as much or as little as you like. The idea is to bring awareness to where you may be feeling excitement or depletion.

- At this point in my life, my connection to God (the Sacred, Divine, whatever word you choose) is best described as...

- This connection is strengthened by...

- I feel most alive when...

- My energy is drained by...

- I am longing for...

When you are finished, give thanks for any new insights that have come.

DAY 3

I Am Healed!

He shall cover you with His feathers,
And under His wings you shall take refuge.
Psalm 91:4 (NKJV)

Ruth, an attractive, sixty-ish African American woman walked into the library at the HIV/AIDS Clinic, beamed a loving smile, doled out hugs, and placed a white linen item on the tiny table we had dubbed the "altar." Nine of us were gathered for the weekly spirituality circle for patients, clinic staff, and volunteers. This circle's topic was "Prayer."

When it came time for those who had brought altar items to share, Ruth unfolded her cloth, which was adorned in various shades of lavender and gold stitching. "This is my prayer shawl," Ruth said. "It is a called a tallit. I am told it is a replica of Queen Esther's." We all admired the beautiful object.

"The engraving on the collar says, 'He shall cover you with His feathers, And under His wings you shall take refuge.'" Wrapping the prayer shawl around herself, Ruth told us, "In Moses' time when they were instructed to go into their tents to pray, many times they did not have a tent available. They would simply cover themselves in their tallits."

Ruth covered her head with the shawl for a moment and then pulled it down, allowing it to rest on her shoulders.

"I was so scared when I was diagnosed," Ruth admitted. Heads bobbed in understanding. "One night I was in such emotional pain I wrapped myself in this shawl and prayed to be sheltered under God's wings." Pausing to collect her thoughts, she continued, "I prayed for healing that night. I prayed, and I felt God's wings around me.

"The next morning I woke up and knew, I am healed. My symptoms may still be here, but I am healed. God has wrapped me with people." She said, "People like Dr. Saag, Rev. Malcolm, the clinic's staff, and this group."

Touched by her words and spirit, I called Ruth to ask if I could share this story. She was glad to know her experience might be helpful to others. Ruth is not stingy with her healing.

"You know, Mary, I am healed," Ruth exclaimed. "Sure, I have symptoms, but I'm healed. God healed me that night. Really, everybody has a part to play in this healing."

"What do you mean?" I asked.

"Well, it's like going to the theater. Dr. Saag, he showed up on the stage years before I needed him. But I see this as very personal. He was there to care for me when I needed him most."

I was intrigued by her concept of a cosmic play and encouraged her to continue.

"That is the power of God," she said. "Things are in place long before we need them." I could imagine Ruth smiling on the other end of the phone, grateful to share her hard-won wisdom.

"When I was diagnosed, I thought the worst. Then I met everyone at the Heartsong Retreat sponsored by the clinic, and I knew, there is gonna be a blessing in this! And there have been blessings—many of them."

Rachel Naomi Remen writes in *My Grandfather's Blessings*, "Sometimes life's power shines through us, even when we do not notice. We become a blessing to others then, simply by being as we are."

PRACTICE

Wrap Yourself in God's Wings

If you have a prayer shawl, bring it with you to your sacred space. If not, find a blanket, towel, anything you would like to designate as your prayer shawl.

Sit quietly with the "shawl" wrapped around you. Breathe. Read this excerpt from Psalm 91:14:

"He will cover you with his feathers,
and under his wings you will find refuge." (NIV)

Imagine your shawl as God's wings wrapped around you, holding you, soothing you, loving you, healing you. Ask for specific healing for something

Day 3: I Am Healed!

that is causing you physical, emotional, or spiritual pain. Stay in this soothing space, wrapped in God's wings for as long as you like.

When you are ready, take a few deep, cleansing breaths and give thanks for the love that always surrounds you. Amen.

DAY 4

Namaste

When we are mirrored in the eyes of someone who loves us and accepts us in our essence, our soul is released.
Marion Woodman

Yoga classes often conclude with teacher and students bowing to one another, palms pressed together in front of the heart, offering the sanskrit greeting, "Namaste." What is this namaste? Originating from the Hindu tradition, the term holds several meanings. My favorite is, "The Divinity within me honors the Divinity within you."

Recently my friend Susan was waiting in a long grocery line. She was tired and so overwhelmed that she was wondering if she might be on the verge of a nervous breakdown. When Susan placed her items on the counter the store clerk asked, "How are you today?"

"You don't really want to know!" she said.

The clerk stopped what he was doing and looked at her directly, sincerely, "Yes I do."

They spent a few moments talking, stopping long enough to truly acknowledge each other. When Susan left the store she was still concerned about how she would manage, but she felt different. She had been blessed by a stranger.

Practice

Offer "Namaste"

What if we offered namaste to those around us, honoring our own divinity and reaching out to touch another's blessedness? Even though we aren't living in a culture where it is common to place our hands in front or our hearts, bow, and say, "namaste," how might we comfortably offer namaste to someone?

Could you simply send a silent namaste to a stranger on the street? Throughout your day, consider staying open to the possibility of honoring that place of divinity in another. How does this silent or spoken gesture move you? Perhaps you will silently breathe a namaste to a friend on the telephone or to someone who is standing in front of you, challenging you in a particularly difficult way. If there are children in your life, you might want to teach them this unusual word and show them how you honor the divinity in them.

Namaste.

DAY 5

Doin' the Hummingbird

Not what we have, but what we enjoy constitutes our abundance.
                                                          Epicurus

MANY MORNINGS, COFFEE CUPS IN hand, Malcolm and I take our seats in the stadium (OK, the Adirondack chairs on the deck) and watch the hummingbird games. Small bodies zip past at top speed, wings flapping at a million beats per second. One will land on the feeder, only to be dive-bombed by another hummingbird or two. We never tire of their mid-air battles. In fact, we mourn their departure in October and anticipate their return in April.

There are six perches and holes on this feeder. If they wanted to, our little friends could ALL sit peacefully and sip the nectar. Imagine the energy they would save NOT fighting, dive-bombing, and playing protector of the perch!

I can't understand why these tiny creatures insist on spending their brief lives battling for food when there is more than enough to go around. I bet a lot of us do the hummingbird dance. Sometimes I imagine God is like Malcolm and me, watching the show and wondering, *Why do they operate from such fear? I have provided them with everything. There is no need to worry, no need to fight. Look, here's a perch; simply drink from the cup of life.*

How much energy would we save if we opened our eyes to the abundance that surrounds us? How much more generous would we be if we weren't worried that someone else might get our "share"?

PRACTICE

Acknowledging Abundance

Make a list of all the ways in which you have been blessed with abundance. You might want to include personal attributes, material things, and meaningful relationships—maybe your surroundings or your work. Don't hold back, make note of anything that comes to mind, even the simple things we tend to take for granted like the sun shining or life-giving rain. After writing your list, take a moment to give thanks. "Thank you for the safety of my home." "I am grateful for the love of my partner." "Thank you sun for rising every day."

You might want to take your abundance experience one step further and identify something from your list to give away or share. You could clean out a closet and give away some clothes to the homeless or invite a friend over for a special meal. You'll know what to do.

DAY 6

Listening Devoutly

Listen with the ear of the heart.

St. Benedict

WE WERE A CIRCLE OF eleven women and one man, bound by a common interest; we wanted to become better spiritual companions. Over the course of the long weekend, we were each given the opportunity to share our spiritual autobiographies.

The guidelines were simple. Only the person telling his or her story could speak; the rest of us were encouraged to listen devoutly. Listening devoutly means tuning out the constant chatter in our busy minds and tuning in to another. This sacred practice requires full attention with all of our senses and intuitive faculties. What is the message beneath the words? How is the speaker's body language congruent, or not, with the spoken communication?

Listening devoutly means resisting the temptation to make a comment, to judge, or to try to "fix" the speaker. Often out of a desire to create connection or show support, we interrupt another with "our story" so that the speaker will know we understand. Inadvertently, when we do this, we truncate the other's story and probably thwart true understanding. And we shift the focus to ourselves. Similarly, when someone risks vulnerability and begins to cry, express frustration, or any other emotion that we find uncomfortable, we may want to ease our own discomfort or make ourselves "needed" by offering solutions when what might be most supportive is a simple, loving presence.

Listening devoutly means bearing witness to another. Within each of us is a unique and powerful story. Rarely do we have the opportunity to share our story without interruption. During the course of the weekend, we each bravely shared our truth—some of us for the first time. Holy silence punctuated these tender stories, drawing us to the their true meaning.

Being listened to devoutly creates trust. Each of us is hungry to be heard and to trust that our story will be treasured as the jewel that it is. When it was my turn, I was surprised at what I said. The supportive, empathetic faces looking back at me coaxed out pieces of my story that longed to be told but that I had not intended to share. By the end of the weekend, strangers had become friends.

Listening devoutly means choosing to understand over choosing to be right. Recently Malcolm and I were eating dinner in our favorite Indian restaurant. Before our Samosas arrived, Malcolm said some things that were challenging for me to hear. My initial reaction was to start crafting a response while he was talking so that I could rebut and be RIGHT. Thankfully, I was fresh from my weekend experience. A still, small voice encouraged me to "just listen."

The tone of the conversation softened immediately. My internal shift somehow created an opening for Malcolm to express difficult truths I didn't want to hear, but needed to know. The more I sought understanding, the more he shared his feelings. A potentially contentious conversation turned into an open discussion of shared concerns, ultimately yielding a new, deeper way of relating. Had I reacted from my reflexive, defensive posture I might have left feeling RIGHT, but certainly not enlightened.

 PRACTICE

Listen Devoutly

At least one time today while in a conversation with another person, preferably in person, but over the telephone can also work, choose to listen devoutly to what the other is saying. What did you notice? How was this different from the way you normally listen?

DAY 7

Shabbat

Sabbath honors the necessary wisdom of dormancy...a period in which we lie fallow, and restore our souls.
Wayne Muller

CAROLINE GIVES HERSELF ONE DAY off each week. A blessed day when she doesn't answer the phone unless she wants to; she reads, prays, naps, watches movies—she does whatever appeals to her, whatever calls to her. Caroline is one of the most spiritually connected and generous people I know. I wonder if there is a correlation between her practice of rest, her connection to the Divine, and her compassionate heart.

In the Jewish tradition, Shabbat is observed from sundown on Friday until the appearance of three stars in the sky on Saturday night. Origins for Shabbat are found in Genesis 2:3: "So God blessed the seventh day and hallowed it, because on it God rested from all the work that he had done in creation" (NRSV).

Shabbat is primarily a day of rest and spiritual enrichment. Special blessings, meals, rest, and certain restrictions are all part of Shabbat. It is a time of remembering. Remembering the gift of creation and remembering that we are free. For the Jewish people, Shabbat also commemorates freedom from slavery in Egypt.

How can we incorporate some form of Shabbat in our own lives? How could we honor the faithfulness of the sun rising each morning and the moon each night? How can we claim our freedom from the rigors of work? Who would we be if we embraced this tradition? Rabbi Harold Kushner remarks, "I would like to think that Sabbath observance, like virtue, is its own reward, that it is worth doing not because it makes you a better worker, but because it makes you a better human being in those parts of your life that have nothing to do with work."

Of course, taking a day off is more difficult for someone with young children, many jobs, an elderly parent. Yet, isn't this soul restoration project particularly important for caregivers? Imagine the message we could give our children if they experienced rest as a natural part of their day. Perhaps they could even participate in planning this special time.

Could you incorporate a ritual of rest in your week? Your day? For many of us, the greatest barriers to rest are an addiction to being busy, to perfectionism, and to not granting ourselves permission.

 PRACTICE

Taking Sabbath

At its best, this exercise requires more than fifteen minutes. Ideally, you will give yourself the gift of an entire day. Perhaps the proposition of an entire day focused on self seems outrageous, selfish even. Have you ever heard the flight attendant's instructions to "place your own oxygen mask on first"? Imagine you are taking this time to breathe in the Spirit.

Carving out your Sabbath may require ingenuity and flexibility. Is there someone who would take your children for at least part of the day? Are there commitments you could postpone or say no to that would open up time? If there are others in the house, how could you incorporate them in the plan? Get their buy-in for some form of renewal.

Set aside an amount of time that will suit your situation, and give yourself the gift of doing only what you want during that period of time. Continually ask yourself what may seem to be the most unnatural of questions: What do I want to do in this moment? Perhaps it will be napping, planting flowers in the garden, reading, making love, or watching a movie. Listen to your heart's desire and respond. Notice how you feel.

When I was on sabbatical Sr. Mary McGehee reminded me of these Sabbath instructions.

1. Rest, rest, rest...do not cook, do not clean, do not walk too far, do not go to the market, do not put a load on your ox, your ass, yourself. Rest, rest, rest.

2. Open your eyes and ears and heart, and look around at all the blessings that surround you. (As God did on the seventh day, and then said: This is good!) Allow yourself to delight in all these glories.

Day 7: Shabbat

3. Acknowledge that you are NOT in charge. The Creator of the Universe is STILL holding all in dynamic love.

Close your Sabbath time with a prayer of thanksgiving and the intention to move into the rhythm of your week with a loving, calm heart.

DAY 8

Truth Telling

Your lies often reveal who you wish you were.
Bella DePaulo

I stepped on the elliptical machine, punched the buttons to begin my workout, and the nosy contraption asked for my weight. I despise this question, but the machine won't start without an answer. Usually I enter a number that is at least five pounds lower than my actual weight. What's the harm?

For some reason, I couldn't type in my "lie" weight. I put in the correct number. My mind raced, keeping pace with my arms and legs.

What's the big deal? I thought. *Who cares if I am putting in my accurate weight?* As I considered this question I realized it matters to me. It's not the machine I am lying to, but myself. I think there are two reasons I lie when I step on the elliptical machine. First, I don't want the guy next to me to know how much I weigh. Second, I like the smaller number. It just feels better.

By perpetuating the lie I am giving myself the message that the way I am isn't good enough—I'm too big. If I am overweight, why not come to terms with it and change my behaviors to address the problem? If I am at a healthy weight, why not embrace it? Two perfectly good choices—neither is available to me when I am lying to myself.

I remember a time when I told myself I was happy working a demanding job that frequently took me away from my children. "I love the freedom and the money and the…" I would say with a smile, while the lie coiled in my gut. Eventually, I landed in the hospital with extreme stomach pain.

Lies—even little ones—take energy and distort reality. I wonder if our manipulations of the mind don't get in the way of the whispers of the Spirit. What might unfold in my life if I were open and honest.

Where else, I wondered, am I lying to myself? Is my elliptical fib a "gateway" lie, a lie that leads to other self-deceptions?

 Practice

Truth Telling

Today, pay attention to the messages you send yourself. Be hyper-vigilant about listening to the "internal chatter." If you "hear" that you're beginning to tell yourself a lie, consider: *What am I trying to avoid?* Make a commitment to counter the small, and maybe not so small, deceptions. What shifts in you when you focus on the truth?

Take time at the end of the day to jot down thoughts about your experience and any possible changes you might want to make.

DAY 9

Naming the Nameless

The Tao that can be told is not the eternal Tao. The Name that can be named is not the eternal Name.

Tao Te Ching

Many mornings I conclude my Centering Prayer time with the Lord's Prayer. Actually, I have taken to amending the prayer. It seems rather arrogant of me, an unschooled layperson, to mess with these sacred words by beginning the prayer with "Loving Creator" instead of "Our Father." But I do it anyway. Also, during worship services, I modify some of the songs and prayers.

Most traditional prayers refer to God as "Father" and "He." I love my father, my husband, and my son, but sometimes I grow weary of all the masculine language we use to describe the Divine. What I worship is greater than "he" or "she." So sometimes I insert "Mother" instead of "Father" or "God" instead of "He." If the language of the Spirit is metaphorical, not literal, why do most of the metaphors point in one direction, toward the masculine?

My favorite term for the unnamable is "Beloved." Rolling off the tongue "Beloved" feels softer, more expansive. And yet, words are inadequate to express the fullness of the Creator, the Imminent Presence.

Lao Tzu, the presumed author of the Tao Te Ching, had the right idea. The moment we begin to name the Nameless, we have diminished this Presence. Yet, we need language to communicate with one another and with ourselves.

According to Islamic tradition, the prophet Muhammad said, "To God belongs 99 names, 100 minus 1; anyone who memorizes them will enter Paradise." Names like "The All Beneficent," "The Most Merciful," "The Creator," "The Ever Forgiving" are recited. Beautiful names. Muslims believe the power lies in the utterance of the words. Understanding is secondary.

Holding the Beloved in our hearts and making ourselves available for union with the Creator is the lifelong path of the contemplative. If naming is a catalyst for this communion, then let's follow our Islamic brothers and sisters and fling the door wide open. Naming is important.

Living AWAKE

 PRACTICE

Naming

Bringing a prayerful presence to your sacred space, light a candle and/or incense and sit in silence for five or ten minutes. Gently consider your favorite names for the Nameless; linger with them, ponder them. If it feels comfortable, say the names aloud, write them down, honor them and praise the Presence they attempt to describe. Perhaps you have never considered the terms "Mother" or "Allah" for God. Take a few more moments to write down or say all of the names that come to mind. Maybe you want to give yourself permission to be silly and use nonsensical, even irreverent names. Finally, ask yourself: How do the words most commonly used for naming the Nameless enhance or diminish my relationship with the Divine? What, if anything, does this tell me about myself, my life experiences, and my relationship with the Nameless?

When you are finished, give thanks. And, of course, feel free to use any names you wish!

DAY 10

Pour Your Heart into It

There exists only the present instant...
a Now which always and without end is itself new.
Meister Eckhart

Several years ago, I took a workshop on Ayurveda, a holistic healing system believed to be over 7,000 years old. Sitting cross-legged on the stage, our teacher, Maya Tiwari (known as Mother Maya), led us in transformative chants one minute and, the next, scolded us about American consumerism and waste. What struck me about Mother Maya was her passion. Whether sitting intently listening to a question or gesturing and sharing a story, she had amazing momentum and animation.

Fascinated by this system for living, I bought her book, *Ayurveda: A Life of Balance*, and learned that the intention (heart) a cook brings to the preparation of a meal impacts the experience for both the cook and those who eat that meal. Although my interest in Ayurveda was short-lived, Mother Maya's teachings have frequently come to mind over the past decade.

When we were living in Tokyo, years after my encounter with Mother Maya, one of our American neighbors gave birth to her third child. I offered to cook pasta shells for the family on the night the mother and her baby returned home from the hospital. Remembering the Ayurvedic teaching, I poured my whole heart into preparing the meal. Dipping my spoon into ricotta cheese, I reached deep within to send blessings to the mother as well as the baby, who would be nourished by this meal through his mother's milk. Stirring the spinach, mozzarella, and ricotta, I held the older sister and brother in my heart—hoping they would receive their new sibling with joy and remember that they were still loved. Finally, spooning pasta sauce over shells, I thought of the father and sent him strength to support his family emotionally as well as financially during this major transition, a long way from home.

Filled with unexpected love for these casual acquaintances, I felt so alive. As I bent over the oven and placed the glass pan into the heat, an unexpected "Amen" fell from my lips. The mundane had become holy.

 Practice

Pour Your Heart into It

Consider something that you will be doing today, maybe an ordinary task like cooking or taking a walk. Think about pouring your whole heart into this activity. How could you approach the experience with passion, like Mother Maya? Is there some way you could send blessings to others as you accomplish this task? Don't hold back. Commit to bringing all of your being to the process—your senses, your emotions, your intelligence. EVERYTHING!

After you have finished your experience, come back to your sacred space and reflect on how pouring your heart into your chosen task/exercise impacted you. Perhaps you'll want to write some thoughts in your journal.

DAY 11

Finding the Center

*Faith is opening and surrendering to God. The spiritual journey
does not require going anywhere because
God is already with us and in us.*

Fr. Thomas Keating

After the death of my dear friend Rhonda, a grief counselor introduced me to the Christian contemplative prayer practice, Centering Prayer. Although I had been meditating for years, my practice felt dead and my connection to God frayed. The counselor thought this practice might awaken something within me that, in my sadness, had gone dormant. I have practiced this prayer nearly every day since.

In the beginning, even though I was drawn to the contemplative qualities of the prayer, I was frustrated sometimes by how my mind would stray like a curious toddler. Results-oriented by nature, I wasn't sure anything was really "happening." Then I heard an encouraging story.

A Catholic nun attending a Centering Prayer workshop offered the following observation to Fr. Thomas Keating, one of the founding members and the spiritual guide of Contemplative Outreach, Ltd.

"Father, I am a failure at this prayer," the nun said. "In twenty minutes I have had at least ten thousand thoughts."

"How lovely!" Fr. Thomas responded without missing a beat. "Ten thousand opportunities to return to God!"

Thanks to the guidance of wise teachers, I have come to understand that the fruit of the Centering Prayer practice is more nuanced than the results-driven approach I often follow in life. Over time, I trust that I will grow in patience, love, kindness, and an ability to surrender my agendas. Taking time for Centering Prayer is helpful in this endeavor.

When our yearning for union with the Divine exceeds the limitations of words, Centering Prayer is a reminder to silently make ourselves available, open, and receptive to God, to life, to love.

 PRACTICE

Centering Prayer

Instructions courtesy of Contemplative Outreach, Ltd.

Take twenty minutes for Centering Prayer. You may wish to continue this practice on a daily basis.

1. Choose a sacred word as the symbol of your intention to consent to God's presence and action within.

2. Sitting comfortably and with eyes closed, settle briefly and silently introduce the sacred word as the symbol of your consent to God's presence and action within.

3. When engaged with your thoughts (including body sensations, feelings, images, and reflections), return ever-so-gently to the sacred word.

4. At the end of the prayer period, remain in silence with eyes closed for a couple of minutes. You may wish to finish with the Lord's Prayer or a spontaneous prayer from your heart.

Day 12

Cultivating Kindness

We need to be angels for each other to give each other strength and consolation. Because only when we fully realize that the cup of life is not only a cup of sorrow, but also a cup of joy will we be able to drink it.

Henri Nouwen

One afternoon Malcolm, a Chaplain at a large hospital, was paged to the Palliative Care Unit to visit a 96-year-old woman who was near death. During his visit, she spoke of her wonderful life, her faith in God, and a peace within even though she knew she would never feel the sun on her face or breathe fresh air again. Her daughter, eyes brimming with sadness and love, hovered nearby. Holding the elderly woman's hands, Malcolm offered a prayer for her and her daughter. Softly, she murmured, "Thank you, God," over and over again. It was as if she were giving thanks for each and every one of those ninety-six years, again and again, "Thank you, God."

In moments like these, Malcolm told me, "it's difficult to determine who is ministering to whom."

A few days later he was paged to the same room because the woman had died and her daughter needed comforting. When Malcolm walked into the room, another woman was holding the daughter, stroking her back. He stayed nearby, trying to offer support without interfering. The visitor whispered a soothing prayer—balm for the daughter's fresh grief. And then she began to sing softly, "Amazing grace how sweet the sound…"

Visibly encouraged, the daughter began to sing along; Malcolm soon joined the chorus.

He wondered, *Who is this angelic visitor? A nurse? A friend?*

At the end of the song, the visitor held the daughter's face in her hands and said, "I know what you are going through, dear woman. My mother is down the hall in one of the rooms, and her breath is getting more shallow by the hour. Any day now she will die, and I will miss my mama so much too."

Then the daughter hugged the visitor and said, "I'm so sorry your mama is dying, I am so, so sorry. It will be okay, I promise, it will be okay."

Daughter to daughter, they comforted each other. One had just lost her mother, the other was about to lose hers. No longer strangers, they were simply sisters in grief.

Practice

Cultivating Kindness

The visitor's story is extraordinary. We are all given opportunities to extend kindness, often in the most ordinary ways. What would it look like if today you set your heart on kindness? At least one time TODAY offer to do something for another person—a family member, a friend, a stranger. Perhaps you could wait and hold the door for a stranger. Or you might call a friend who is going through a hard time. Wouldn't it be fun to buy fresh flowers and give them to someone who has been generous to you?

Lavish the world with kindness. Why stop at one act? Today, notice how frequently the world offers you opportunities for benevolence. Drink in the warmth of blessings bestowed upon you, the blesser.

DAY 13

The Light of
Impermanence

*The Master observes the world but trusts her inner vision. She
allows things to come and go. Her heart is open as the sky.*
Lao Tzu

EIGHT YEARS AGO MALCOLM FULFILLED a childhood dream by moving to a home on a lake. Three years later, Brendan, Kiki, and I joined him. We are blessed—with birds that serenade us as we drink coffee and big starry nights. It is serene. It is also very far from work and friends and just about everything. We love this home *and* we are tired of spending so much time in the car. After much discussion, we have decided to let the lake house go and move to a simpler life, closer to work and easier to maintain. Framed by the truth that we may not live here much longer, we are enjoying the lake house more this summer than we have since we first moved here. Now, the sunsets seem more brilliant, the hawk's call more piercing. We want to fully appreciate all the lake's gifts.

Life is always changing. Sometimes the changes happen because of choices we make, like selling our home. Other times, it is an unwelcome event like a diagnosis, a death, or a failed endeavor that brings change.

It is interesting that the *Tao Te Ching* equates being open-hearted with a willingness to allow things to come and go. Appreciating what I do have, embracing life with an open heart, honoring each precious breath—how I long to live like the Master. Focusing on breathing can help us embrace the gifts of now.

 PRACTICE

Conscious Breathing

Sit comfortably with your spine straight, but not rigid. Close your eyes and lay your palms face up on your thighs in receiving mode. Breathe at your normal pace with your mouth closed. On your inhalation notice the air entering your nostrils. Follow your breath as it moves down your trachea, into your chest, and, finally, through your belly. Then, follow that breath back up until it leaves your nostrils. Continue this cycle of silently following your breath for five to ten minutes.

When you are finished rest for a moment or two, give thanks for your breath, open your eyes, and enjoy your breath-filled day.

DAY 14

Technology Sabbatical

For it is only framed in space that beauty blooms.
Anne Morrow Lindbergh

"THEY WERE ALL SITTING AROUND in the back yard, texting other kids who weren't there." My friend Dorothy gasped, describing her teenage daughter and her daughter's friends' behavior. "It was bizarre. They weren't talking to each other at all, just texting away on their phones."

We shook our heads in wonder at this new generation and their gadget-laden lives. Yet, it isn't only the "kids" who seem to have trouble creating techno-boundaries.

That very same night, Kiki came into the family room talking to me about her day at work. I half-heartedly listened, busy replying to emails on my laptop. Frustrated, she stood up and said, "Well, I guess I'll go downstairs to watch TV." I wanted to snatch her back and apologize—ask for a "do over." It was too late; the moment was lost.

One night when Malcolm and I were enjoying a romantic dinner at our favorite restaurant, I asked him a question. He didn't know the answer and pulled out his "smartphone." My jaw dropped.

"What are you doing?" I asked

"I'm answering your question. Why?" He seemed hurt.

"Please put that thing away," I quipped.

Thankfully we can now laugh about our experience that evening.

It is hard to believe that only twenty-five years ago many people did not have personal computers at their desks; just fifteen years ago email began to be widely used; and the Blackberry's popularity is only five years old. How did we survive without all of this "help"?

Like most things, technology has both a light and a dark side. Used appropriately, it does increase our ability to connect; it can also be the cause of major disconnect.

Technology Sabbatical

Okay, this is not an easy task for most of us, but it can be illuminating. Choose a period of time, ideally an entire day, when you will not check email, use your cell phone (unless in an emergency), or watch TV. Make a commitment not to use any technology at all. What will you do with this newly-created space in your life? Maybe you'd like to savor a quiet walk in the woods. Perhaps lingering at a bookstore would be refreshing. Listen, truly listen without distraction to another. Create something inviting that you want to move toward as you move away from over-stimulation and the instant gratification of technology.

I am not proposing we throw our technology away and go back to the 1950s. I am merely suggesting blocking off a period of time—half a day, a day, even an entire weekend—when we choose not to use some or all of our technological devices. Imagine what might bloom in that fertile ground of unfettered time.

At the end of your techno-free time, consider: What did you experience? Do you want to set boundaries around your use of technology? Make a list of your favorite non-technological activities.

DAY 15

Thank-a-Thon

To receive everything, one must open one's hands and give.
Taisen Deshimaru

RIDING BIKES WITH HER SISTER up and down their long driveway, climbing moss-draped pecan trees, and wading in creeks are some of my friend Jenny's fondest memories. These activities were healthy diversions from her unpredictable life. Jenny's mother had bipolar disorder. During the good times, "Mama" would laugh, and sing, and spring to life. During the bad times, a devout Jewish physician named Dr. Friedman would come to their rural Mississippi home and tend to Jenny's mom, kindly enduring the woman's evangelizing and ranting that was intended to "save" him. He always departed without leaving a bill.

When Jenny was in the tenth grade, her mother's health declined to the point that Jenny was sent to live at Baptist Children's Village (BCV), a children's home. Leaving the home and family she loved was like having the sun snatched from Jenny's sky. She was required to line up for intrusive body inspections and haircuts, among other indignities.

BCV's girls' choir traveled throughout Mississippi, performing in Baptist churches to raise money. When the choir director, Miss Nix, first heard Jenny sing, she waived the mandatory waiting period for joining the choir and featured her as a soloist. The other girls were jealous, but Jenny didn't care; she loved singing and being near Miss Nix.

On Sundays, the girls would load into the back of the van, on benches along the sides. Miss Nix always sat in the front and the girl who lined up first to get on the van was allowed to sit next to her. Jenny ached to sit next to Miss Nix. She packed up early on choir days in hopes of being first. Miss Nix would then let Jenny put her head on her lap as she softly caressed her hair and murmured loving encouragement. Jenny anticipated time with Miss Nix the way children wait for Santa Claus. Miss Nix made life at the home bearable, shining a warm light of love on all of her girls.

Today Jenny is a successful motivational speaker with the moniker, "Alabama's funniest lady." Her life is good; she is surrounded by love. Recently she was reading Rachel Naomi Remen's, *My Grandfather's Blessings*. Memories of Dr. Friedman's generosity and Miss Nix's kindness flooded back to Jenny. She felt deep gratitude and wanted to let those who had carried her know—the seeds they had planted in her had blossomed, like wildflowers. She was now teaching others what they had taught her.

Jenny decided to drive back to Mississippi on a self-proclaimed, "Thank-a-Thon."

Miss Nix's home was her first stop. Opening the door, Miss Nix (now a recently widowed Mrs. Goodwin) crooned, "You are a drink a fresh water for me." They sat in her home, sipping sweet tea and reminiscing. Jenny thanked Mrs. Goodwin for acknowledging her talent, told her that she was the first person to "hear her voice." When Jenny described how much it meant to lay her head on her lap, Mrs. Goodwin's eyes filled with tears.

"You remember that?" she asked.

"I'll never forget it as long as I live," Jenny beamed.

Next stop, Dr. Friedman.

Practice

Giving Thanks

Each of us has been touched by the kindness of others. Consider a pivotal time in your life when the kindness, generosity, or encouragement of another had an impact on you. Maybe there was a coach who saw previously unrecognized talent in you or a neighbor who held you when you were grieving; perhaps someone lent you money. There are probably countless examples. What was the situation? Who helped you? How? Share your thoughts in your journal or simply sit and enjoy remembering another's kindness with gratitude.

Is there some way you can connect with this person? Would you like to call or write and share how much she helped you, how her generosity lives on in you today? If you can't make contact either because of distance or death, is there some way you would like to honor this kind being?

DAY 16

Befriending Emotions

Compassion arises when we meet pain and suffering with love.
Beth Roth

"Registration is way up," Erin told me. She was the program coordinator who had booked me for an upcoming workshop. "This is the largest crowd we've had for this event in a long time!"

I should have been thrilled, but I was terrified. What if my talk wasn't any good? What if the audience was bored? What if I forgot what I was going to say? What if...? What if...? What if...? And none of those "What if's" was encouraging.

Gripped, I was unable to work on my speech. My brain froze like a car battery in a Calgary winter. Staring at the blank page before me, I felt my throat tighten and breath shorten. After sitting paralyzed for a spell, I suddenly remembered the teachings from Buddhist and Christian teachers to "lean into" afflictive emotions. My head told me, *Run like a cheetah on the Svengali.* My heart said, *Lean in; lean in.*

Listen to your heart, I told myself. I took a few moments to practice the Christian contemplative Welcoming Prayer. I closed my eyes and focused on the sensation in my body, the tightening in my chest. I sat with that for a while. Then I named the sensation "fear" and welcomed the Divine Indwelling* into that fear, silently repeating, *Welcome Fear. Welcome Fear.* Slowly the vice in my chest loosened as I continued consenting to the Divine Indwelling; I WELCOMED the fear until the sensation of fear subsided. Finally, I let go by repeating, *I let go of the desire for security; I let go of the desire for affection; I let go of the desire for control. I let go of the desire to change this sensation.*

After a few moments of silence, I opened my eyes and approached composing my speech with a bit more equanimity, a tad more self-awareness.

Leaning into our emotions is the exact opposite of trying to "positive think" our way out of difficult emotions or pain. If we can listen for the wisdom of our emotions, stay with them, and ride their turbulent waves, eventually they reach the shore and dissolve into the sand.

PRACTICE

Welcoming Prayer

The Welcoming Prayer is best experienced "in the moment" of difficult emotions/sensations. However, if you sit for a few minutes and remember something in your life that is causing a degree of physical or emotional pain, like a difficult relationship or chronic bodily pain, you may practice this prayer even when you are not in "immediate need" of it. By practicing you will be able to call on this tool when you are in the heat of the moment.

Instructions courtesy of Contemplative Outreach, Ltd.

Movement One: FOCUS, feel, and sink into the feelings, emotions, thoughts, sensations, and commentaries in your body.

Movement Two: WELCOME the Divine Indwelling in the feelings, emotions, thoughts, commentaries, or sensations in your body by saying, "Welcome."

Movement Three: LET GO by repeating the following sentences:

"I let go of my desire for security; I let go of my desire for affection; I let go of my desire for control. I let go of the desire to change this feeling, sensation, or situation."

Sit in silence and, if you like, close with a prayer.

*In the Christian contemplative world, Divine Indwelling is used to identify the Holy Trinity present within each of us. If "Divine Indwelling" is an uncomfortable concept for you, feel free to exchange it for a term that signifies, for you, a connection to God or a Higher Power.

DAY 17

Reclaiming

A great calamity is not to have failed, but to have failed to try.
Unknown

YEARS AGO I WAS AN adventurer, backpacking in Yellowstone and biking long distances. My motto seemed to be, "Work hard. Play hard." Like many of us, over time my weekend pursuits became more and more domesticated. Pushing my children on neighborhood park swings replaced trekking through the wilderness.

One of my favorite memories is of a hike to Heart Lake in Yellowstone. Three friends and I had tromped in eight miles to our destination, leaving civilization late in the afternoon. The hike was more difficult than we had expected. What should have taken three hours stretched into a grueling five-hour journey. Early in the hike, rain began to fall. We pulled out our ponchos and silently trudged toward our destination. Setting up camp in the dark drizzle was hardly what any of us had hoped for when we planned our trip.

The next morning I rolled out of my sleeping bag and pulled back the tent flap to a stunning sight. Only a few yards away, steam gently rose above the crystal blue water of Heart Lake. The protective backdrop of Mt. Sheridan hovered on the other side of the lake, her snowy reflection mirrored on the still water.

Quietly, so as not to disturb my companions, I started a fire and made coffee. When the black brew was ready, I poured it into my tin cup and sat on a log, peacefully soaking up the majestic vision. My wool-gloved hands gripping the tin cup, I breathed in the sharp aroma and warmth, a double dose of healing. Graceful geese skimmed the water, dancing in formation. I especially appreciated the harmonious peace given our struggles to reach this now-glorious destination.

These days, I usually make a rather tame hike to the coffee pot—my greatest obstacle being a hungry yellow Lab. Cup in hand, I settle into my comfy chair. This too is a good life, if maybe a little too cushy.

Lately, I have noticed a hesitancy in myself about venturing out and taking risks. I have wondered if reclaiming some of that woman at Heart Lake wouldn't open me to embracing new challenges in my life today. A few weeks ago I bought new hiking boots. Kiki and I explored the Desoto Falls area in northern Alabama. Malcolm and I rented mountain bikes and rode down a steep mountain. The views and the treacherous drops thrilled us.

Surely my pursuits at forty-seven won't be as daring as those at twenty-seven. Yet I want to reclaim the adventurer in me. Not all adventures need to be physical, of course. As I reclaim that woman by the lake, how will other aspects of my life be transformed? How will I be transformed?

 PRACTICE

Reclaiming

Take a few minutes and think back to a time in your life when you felt most alive. What was it about this period that was particularly exciting? What aspect of this self would you like to reclaim? Is there a part of you that you have (either consciously or inadvertently) shut down, ignored, denied?

What one thing could you do to begin reclaiming this part of yourself? How could you take one step in that direction today? Go for it!

DAY 18

Savin' Ain't Lovin'

You have no control over what the other guy does. You only have control over what you do.

A. J. Kitt

THE OTHER EVENING I WAS having dinner with a group of people. Someone at the table suggested I might be able to help an organization that was in great need. One of the women jokingly placed her hand in front of her mouth to cover her words and whispered to me, "You don't have to be the savior…don't save them!"

I thought of when Brendan and Kiki were younger and I would frequently want to rescue them from feeling any hurt or pain. Shouldn't I, their mother, protect them? But sometimes my protecting went well beyond what was healthy for them or for me.

I remember a time when Brendan and Kiki were freshmen in a new high school, and Brendan was playing football. Kiki wasn't involved in a sport that season. Besides her brother Brendan, she didn't know anyone at the school. Kiki wanted me to come and pick her up and hang out with her in town until after his practice was over, when I'd drive them both home.

For the first week I accommodated Kiki, feeling proud that she needed me in this way. But it didn't take long for me to resent the time spent in a coffee shop waiting when I had so many other things I could be doing. The next week I informed Kiki she would have to find something to do on campus until Brendan was finished. She was angry and apprehensive. As dismissal time rolled around on the first day of our new schedule, I felt a vice squeezing my stomach; every inch of my being wanted to swoop in and save my daughter from loneliness. I imagined her all alone, uncomfortable and scared.

When I picked them up at 5:30, Kiki seemed fine but would not admit anything positive about her experience. By the end of the week, she had found a cadre of girls to hang out with; four years later they were her closest friends.

This experience with Kiki taught me that the line between being support-ive and standing in the way of another's growth can be razor thin. Also, I realized that my need to be the savior said much about my desire to be needed and to control situations.

PRACTICE

Trusting Another

Take a few minutes to reflect: Is there someone or some organization that you repeatedly feel the need to save? If so, sit with these questions for as long as possible. Ask yourself:

Why don't I trust the other to be able to solve problems on his or her own?

What am I afraid will happen if I don't offer deliverance?

What need am I trying to fill by being the savior?

How could I do this differently?

Be gentle with yourself and the other.

Imagine approaching this relationship from a different place, finding a new way of loving. Close with a prayer of your own, or you might use, "Thank you for the gift of _____ in my life. Grant me wisdom and guidance in this relationship. May I trust _____ to make healthy choices. When _____ experiences difficulty, may I have the strength to support and encourage without controlling. May _____ and I create a new way of relating that is empowering for all. Amen."

DAY 19

Love God, Love Neighbor

Love the Lord your God with all your heart and all your soul, and with all your mind. This is the first and greatest commandment. And the second is like it: Love your neighbor as yourself.

Matthew 22:37–39

In *My Grandfather's Blessings*. Rachel Naomi Remen describes a teaching from the Kabbalah, the mystical teachings of Judaism: "at some point in the beginning of things, the Holy was broken up into countless sparks, which were scattered throughout the universe. There is a god spark in everyone and in everything, a sort of diaspora of goodness."

Some people have done such a clever job of covering up their goodness that for us to find a nugget of "god spark" in them is like digging for a single diamond in a 600-acre field.

But dig we must.

Wouldn't it be wonderful if we were surrounded only by people we got along with? People who affirmed us, agreed with us, made us feel substantial. What an easy life that would be! Not realistic though.

Dig for the treasures we must.

I want to mine this "god spark" in me and be so bold as to help others find it in themselves.

Practice

Walking Meditation

This meditation is adapted by Rev. Mary Earle from a mantra spoken by the Christian desert mothers and fathers.

If possible, take time outdoors, preferably in a peaceful, natural setting. This practice also works well for a labyrinth walk. Before you begin, breathe in a prayer of gratitude. Slowly place your left foot on the ground, thinking or saying out loud, "Love God." When you intentionally place your right foot on the ground think or say, "Love Neighbor." As you walk, slowly repeat with each footfall, "Love God...Love Neighbor....Love God....Love Neighbor... Love God...Love Neighbor...Love God...Love Neighbor..." When you are finished take a few deep breaths and give thanks.

DAY 20

Bestowing Our Blessings

Once blessed, we are blessed forever.
Rachel Naomi Remen

BRENDAN AND KIKI WERE LYING on the carpet outside our guest room, trying to see what was happening through the space under the door. Joined by a few fellow monks and nuns, Lama Norlha Rinpoche—a Tibetan Buddhist monk who was staying with us—was chanting his morning ritual. Brendan and Kiki adored Lama Norlha, especially his childlike nature that belied his sixty-plus years. As I was running up the stairs to reprimand the kids for spying, one of the monks opened the door and invited the three of us to join them.

We all sat cross-legged on the floor as the ritual continued. Ani Palmo, one of the nuns, explained to us in English what they were saying in Tibetan. At the end of the chanting, I started rounding up the kids. "Come on you guys. Time to get ready for school." Lama Norlha interrupted me and called my children over to him. Lama placed his hands on Brendan's cheeks and leaning forward, touched his forehead to Brendan's. Smiling, he repeated the gesture with Kiki. They beamed, feeling his silent and tender blessing.

Years later, Rabbi Rami Shapiro was visiting on a Friday night. I asked if he would lead us in a Shabbat service. Graciously he agreed. Somewhere in the mix of blessing the wine and bread and lighting candles, Rami looked at me and said, "It is customary for you to bless your children at this point in the service." How crazy that I had never thought to do this before. These beloved children of mine had been at my table many a Friday night, and it never entered my mind to close out the week by placing my hands on their heads and giving thanks for them in this special way, to ask for God's protection and blessing upon them.

Self-consciously, I stood and placed my hands on Brendan's head. I gave thanks for the gift of this child, grateful that we belonged to each other and especially to God. Then I turned toward Kiki, placing my palms on her head.

Every morning and every night I pray for Brendan and Kiki. But this outward manifestation of my inward feelings gave Brendan, Kiki, and me the chance to experience blessing together.

Practice

Blessing

Who would you like to bless? Could you, today, lay your hands on her head and acknowledge her sacredness? What words of thanks do you want to give for the blessed in your life? What special blessing would you like to bestow? I encourage you to take a risk, to bless another. This outward manifestation of what we hold dear in our hearts has power and gives meaning in ways we may never completely comprehend.

Blessings to you and yours.

DAY 21

Wonder and Awe

When one flower blooms spring awakens everywhere.
John O'Donohue

Tail wagging, Daisy charged ahead of me on the long, gravel driveway. Realizing we were not stopping at the mailbox but going for the treasured W-A-L-K, she burst into a head-waggling, booty-shaking circle dance punctuated by a leap in the air. How could I help but smile?

This morning the sky offered more questions than answers. To our right, waves of sea-foam clouds floated peacefully. Directly overhead lurked an ominous sheet of gray, and not far to the left, the promise of clear blue bliss.

How do those beautyberry bushes transform overnight from green-leafed shrubs to purple-jeweled feasts for the eye, I wondered as we walked. I remember the first time I saw a beautyberry on an "escape from the world" weekend with my friend Elinor. Coming across this plant, in the middle-of-nowhere-Alabama, is a reminder for me of precious moments with a dear far-away friend.

Dark clouds rumbling, Daisy and I took our chances and carried on. I was almost hoping for drops of rain to arouse my skin. Today, like every day, God was creating something new. Would I have the eyes to see it?

 Practice

Appreciate Nature

As the wise Benedictine Sister Mary McGehee once reminded me years ago: "Take time each day to live in wonder and awe of God's creation."

Many of us have more cement than natural beauty in our midst. If that's the case for you, finding the wonder and awe of creation may seem difficult. When we lived in noisy, crowded Tokyo, exquisite little gardens grew on minuscule parcels of land. Harried "salary men," as middle-class workers were called, would often take a moment or two to stop and marvel at my neighbor's blossoming cherry tree on their way to the train station. I watched them from my window.

I encourage you to explore nature, with all your senses attuned to wonder and awe. Perhaps you could remain open to one item that draws you in a particularly meaningful way—a pinecone perfect in its symmetry, a sweet-smelling rose, a sky of puffy clouds.

Do you live in driving distance of a berry-picking patch?

"I love seeking and picking wild blackberries in the summer and muscadines in the fall," my friend Betty told me. "They are tasty reminders of God's abundant gifts. Even the blackberry thorns and brambles teach me that sometimes the way is hard but that promised rewards are there with the struggle."

Whether it is noticing a city tree, traipsing through a blackberry patch, or enjoying a dewy morning walk, give yourself extended Sabbath time to commune with nature. I encourage you to take at least ten minutes of intentional time outdoors. Three hours, if you can! Breathe in the air, notice the sky, watch a bird in flight, admire a shrub. Invite wonder and awe into your life. Let yourself absorb the abundance of the Creator.

DAY 22

Ya Get What Ya Give

Just remember, you're gonna get what ya give.
Frances Hargraves

A FEW YEARS AGO I had the privilege of briefly knowing Frances Hargraves. Mrs. Hargraves had been teaching school in Chapel Hill, North Carolina, since the sidewalks were made of dirt. She was an anchor in the classroom during the Civil Rights era and was beloved by students of all races. She was known for her willingness to go out of her way for students, family, and friends. So great was her impact on the Chapel Hill community that a middle school and community center were named in her honor.

Weeks before she died, I went to visit her. I wanted to see her one more time and thank her for helping me start a non-profit organization called Project Compassion. Walking into her bedroom with a freshly picked bouquet of black-eyed Susans, I found Mrs. Hargraves surrounded by young family members anxious to attend her. I thanked her for allowing me, a recent acquaintance, the chance to see her when so many wanted to be with her. She smiled and made me feel as though I were the most important visitor in weeks.

When one of the young women commented on all the visitors and flowers Mrs. Hargraves had received, I mentioned that I wasn't surprised. Smiling, Mrs. Hargraves sighed deeply, laid her head back on a pile of pillows and said, "Well chil' ya get what ya give. Just remember, you're gonna get what ya give."

What am I giving? I asked myself.

 PRACTICE

How Do I Want to Be Remembered?

Imagine you are gravely ill, perhaps even on your deathbed. Who would want to come to your bedside to visit you? To give you thanks? What specific things would you want to be remembered for having given to your family, friends, the greater community? How do you want to be remembered?

Take a few moments to reflect on your current life, the way you spend your days. Does the way you invest your time and energy coincide with the way you want to be remembered? What are you giving that you want to continue to give? What would you like to offer that you have withheld? Can you open your heart and give this with love and joy?

Remember, all that we offer, say, and do *today* is how we will be remembered *tomorrow*.

DAY 23

Feed Your Soul

Spirituality does demand attention, mindfulness, regularity, and devotion. It asks for some small measure of withdrawal from a world set up to ignore soul.

Thomas Moore

our copy
Care of the
Soul

In *Care of the Soul*, Thomas Moore reminds us, "Getting away from the world has always been a part of the spiritual life….Some concrete, physical expression of retreat could be the beginning of a spiritual life that would nourish the soul. It could take the modest form of a drawer where dreams and thoughts are kept. It could consist of five minutes in the morning dedicated to writing down the night's dream or to reflect on the day ahead. It might be the decision to take a walk through the woods instead of touring the shopping mall….the soul might benefit most when its spiritual life is performed in the context it favors—ordinary daily vernacular life."

When Brendan and Kiki were young I felt I was losing myself to motherhood. A wise friend counseled me to create a "Feed Your Soul Journal." Each day I would write down what I did to nourish that which was crying out from deep within me. The entries were simple: drinking a latte on the bench near the bird feeder, walking our black Lab, Boomer, alone, going outside while my husband did the dishes. Some of these activities were new. Many were not. Considering what I wanted and needed and taking the time to notice that I was feeding my soul, helped me find myself again. I sought silence, the fertile ground from which the Sacred springs.

Practice

Feed Your Soul

I invite you to give yourself the gift of a "modest form of retreat," a "small measure of withdrawal." Sit in silence for a few minutes and ask yourself, "What might I do today that would feed my soul?" Perhaps you'd like to start a Feed My Soul Journal. Enjoy some quiet time for a few extra minutes so that you can connect with that still, small voice inside. What is it telling you? Can you honor the wisdom of that inner voice and respond by following the actions it whispers to you? Notice small soul gifts in your life. Try to check in with that inner voice as you go through your day. Maybe you would like to return to your sacred space at the end of the day and reflect on your experience.

DAY 24

Welcoming the Stranger

For I was hungry and you gave me food, I was thirsty and you gave me something to drink, I was a stranger and you welcomed me.
Matthew 25:35 (NRSV)

Nestled in my favorite green chair, warmed by the fire and Miss White's hand-sewn quilt, I was enjoying an unusually peaceful evening alone. Suddenly the stillness was shattered by a low, snarling growl from Daisy. Hesitantly, I stood up to turn on the outside light and spotted the object of Daisy's over-zealous protection, a raccoon swinging from one of the bird feeders on the deck.

My involuntary reaction was disgust. Those stupid raccoons make such a mess. Ugh! What a waste of birdseed. I was about to shoo the intruder away when I paused for an instant. Instead of a messy pest I noticed a sweet face staring back at me. I returned his gaze. Stillness hovered under the moon-lit sky as we silently watched one another. Looking into his eyes, I began to soften. Where there had been repulsion, I began to feel attraction. Moments before, yelling at the raccoon seemed the most appropriate response; now that I "knew" him, raising my voice in disgust felt like cruel treatment of a fellow creature.

Enchanted by his masked face and calm response to my presence, I smiled and went inside for the camera. The raccoon stared straight into the camera, compliant as I clicked away. I couldn't wait to show Malcolm the photos of our late-night visitor.

 Practice

Welcoming the Stranger

Many of us have an initial apprehension when we encounter strangers or someone who feels different from us. How do you respond to strangers? Take some time to reflect on a recent encounter with someone new or different.

Were you welcoming, trusting, curious? Or were you frightened by their difference? It can seem natural to judge or ridicule customs and cultures unlike our own. Is that how you responded? Are you naturally curious about those who are different?

As you spend a few minutes considering your feelings about strangers or people you think of as "strange," notice your natural tendencies toward those who are unfamiliar. There are no "right" or "wrong" answers here, only honest observations.

If you would like to develop a habit of welcoming, I encourage you to try one of these exercises. In the course of your day, look for, or create, an opportunity to reach out to someone you would normally keep at bay. Maybe you could go out of your way to smile at or speak to someone you would otherwise ignore. Perhaps there is someone in your life whom you have avoided getting to know; might you want to contact that person and reach out?

We are all "the stranger" at one time or another. Enjoy the opportunity to "welcome the stranger" and be open to what unfolds.

DAY 25

A Selfish Gift

*The weak can never forgive. Forgiveness is the
attribute of the strong.*

Mahatma Gandhi

Forgiving those who have harmed us can feel like pushing a boulder uphill. For me, resentment resides in the gut. I find myself reliving an unkind word, an abuse, a missed opportunity for someone to show me kindness. For many of us our solar plexus tightens, trying to protect us from the pain. But the pain is there, as real as the air we breathe. Sometimes, all we breathe is our pain.

Small transgressions can be easy to forgive, especially when the other party sincerely seeks forgiveness. But the big ones—infidelity, a parent who seemed uncaring, a child who steals from his own mother—these can take years of hard work to move past. And if the one who hurt us shows no remorse, the challenge is even more difficult.

We can pretend we aren't hurt, bury the betrayals in the backyards of our hearts. But every once in a while, something will trigger a cramping in our guts and in our hearts.

Advice columnist Ann Landers used to say, "Hanging onto resentment is letting someone you despise live rent-free in your head."

Recently, I was with a friend discussing a difficult situation that happened months earlier. I had been deeply hurt by someone whom I love. I thought I had completely forgiven this person, but I shocked my friend—and myself—when I blurted out a smarmy, unkind comment about the offending person. It was as if I had no control over my mouth. Pain poured forth in a poisonous spew. Rather than providing relief, my caustic words increased my sadness. Not only was I hurt; I was also being ugly.

Forgiveness is a gift to give, not only to the other party but to ourselves.

Having walked the resentment road before, I realized my behavior was a warning sign that I was harboring untended anger and grief. Pushing it down further would only lead to another untimely eruption. I had work to do. My first order of business was to say the Forgiveness Prayer below because it reminds me of my transgressor's inherent humanity and of my ability to bless.

 Practice

Forgiveness Prayer

Call to mind someone with whom you have had particular difficulty showing forgiveness. It could be someone living or dead. Take time to imagine this person sitting across from you—imagine a look, a smell. Capture the "essence." After a few minutes, repeat this prayer as many times as you like. Depending upon the depth of your pain, you may find you need to pray this prayer only one time or you may return to it daily for years before you feel a sense of release. Call on a Higher Power to be with you in this fruitful and difficult practice. Trust that peace will come.

Forgiveness Prayer by Rev. Dr. Alla Bozarth

I bless you
I release you

I let you be
I let me be

I set you free
I set me free.

When you are finished, sit quietly for a few minutes.

DAY 26

Silencing the Inner Critic

Deliver me, oh Giver of Breath and Life, from the fears that beset me; help me confront the inner shadows...They distract me from all that I yearn to be, and hinder the awakening of hidden gifts that I long to share with others.
Psalm 140, *Psalms for Praying* by Nan C. Merrill

"WHAT HAPPENED TO YOU?" MY friend Marjorie asked. "Last time I saw you, you were so clear. Today, you are all over the place."

Marjorie was right; my energy was scattered and my focus blurry. After a week filled with too much work, too many evenings out, and not enough silence, I was reverting to old, unhealthy ways of thinking.

"It is like the real you has vacated the premises," Marjorie added, "and your inner critic is holed up in your head indulging herself like a drunken rock star."

I cackled at her analogy—a well-needed release from the swamp of negativity I had been slogging through.

What had happened to me? I wondered.

Grateful for my friend's honest and loving comments, I used them as motivation to consider what had precipitated this free-fall into worry and doubt. Busy with travel, work, and volunteer commitments, I had pushed aside my daily Centering Prayer practice for over a week. I couldn't remember the last time I had gone so long without inviting the silence.

Instead of taking time each day to commune with the Beloved, I had been conversing with the "critic." Oh, the critic really is a persistent, clever, and cruel companion. When feeling healthy and balanced, I usually do a pretty good job of recognizing her and dismissing her harmful banter. Without the foundation of my prayer practice in my daily routine, I had allowed her diatribes to dominate. "You look old." "You need to work harder." "You should be saving more money…feeding the homeless…visiting the sick…studying more…"

Marjorie's observation helped me become aware that I was giving my relentless critic free reign—she was squelching my creativity and distracting me from "all that I yearn to be."

After further reflection I decided I would start from a place of "can" and "could," not "shame" and "should." I understood that the critic, though sometimes useful, is not the voice of love. Hers is the voice of limitation. I knew it was time for me to silence the critic and to invite in the Beloved, the voice that marvels at the essence of our true nature, urges us to embrace possibility, and encourages us to offer all of who we are as a gift to ourselves and the world.

Practice

Silencing the Inner Critic

Bring your journal to your sacred space and after a few minutes answer these questions.

Step 1: What does the voice that plants seeds of doubt and limitation say to me? What are the "hot button" issues that send me into a tailspin, questioning my innate worth and beauty? Simply make a list.

Step 2: Invite the presence of the Beloved to be with you as you consider, "How do I let this voice inhibit my offering all of who I am to the world?" Let yourself respond—no filters, no judging. Simply write.

Step 3: What has listening to this voice cost me and others?

Step 4: Ask yourself, "Do I want to allow this voice to have power over how I perceive myself and choose to live my life?"

Step 5: NOTICE AND RELEASE. If the answer to Step 4 is no, conjure up one of the classic "rants" you will hear from this voice. Tune in and listen for only as long as you wish. NOTICE how you feel in your body, then invite God's presence and action to be with you. Imagine releasing the critical voice into the air. Allow the voice to get farther and farther away, softer and softer, until at last it is silent.

Step 6: Close with this prayer. "Beloved Creator, thank you for the many gifts you have bestowed upon me. I draw strength knowing You are as close as every breath I breathe. Thank you for the wisdom and guidance to notice when fear and doubt creep into my heart and for the courage to follow your voice—the voice of Love. It is my heartfelt desire to joyfully offer the gifts you have given me to share. Amen."

DAY 27

Cleanliness Is Overrated

The work will wait while you show the child the rainbow,
but the rainbow won't wait while you do the work.
Patricia Clafford

Like most teenagers, Brendan treasures his sleep. Even though his bedroom has a view of the lake, he usually leaves his blinds closed all day so that he won't forget to pull them down at night. This and his habit of leaving his bed unmade have never been well received by me. Frankly, I have nagged him about his dark and messy room.

When I came home from dropping Brendan off at college, I opened the blinds, swept his room, changed the sheets, and made the bed. Somehow I hoped cleaning would allay my sadness.

Although gratifying for my compulsive and tidy self, the project left me feeling empty. Yes, the blue comforter that had never before stayed on top of the bed matched the wall color perfectly. And yes, the light streaming through the windows seemed to brighten the whole upstairs. But the space didn't feel like Brendan's room. It was way too sterile, lifeless. Nothing about this newly-cleaned room reflected Brendan—the fun he'd had in there with his buddies, talking and playing games; the late nights studying for a test; the sleeping in on Saturday mornings. No dirty clothes, no overflowing trash, no Xbox controllers strewn about.

That night when Malcolm and I went to bed, Kiki said, "I miss Brendan. This is when we'd usually hang out. I'm gonna watch a movie in his room."

In the morning, Kiki and I were leaving for a rare mother/daughter shopping trip. Before heading to the car, I walked into Brendan's room and found a wrinkled comforter, Kiki's dirty socks, a plate with crumbs on the bed, and a half-full glass of chocolate milk sitting on the wooden floor. My first impulse was to fuss at Kiki and make her clean up the mess before we got in the car. I resisted that urge and simply closed the bedroom door so we could leave on a good note. Our day was filled with laughter that I especially treasure now that Kiki, too, is no longer living at home.

That night I opened the door to Brendan's room and was grateful to Kiki for re-humanizing the space.

PRACTICE

Leave a Mess

At least once today, forego a cleaning project. Instead, use the time you would have spent cleaning relating to someone. Decide to leave the dishes in the sink and call an old friend; drop the broom and play on the floor with your toddler; or cruise past that stack of messy papers on your way out for a walk with the dog. Bring yourself fully to the alternative activity and NOTICE the experience.

DAY 28

What Do I Love?

Each today, well lived, makes yesterday a dream of happiness and each tomorrow a vision of hope. Look, therefore, to this one day for it and it alone is life.

Sanskrit poem

When my friend Jacob was going through a divorce, he realized that for the first time in sixteen years he was making decisions all on his own. He felt "locked-up" about how to spend his free time. What did he love doing? How did he want to spend the weekend? He couldn't believe how long it had been since he'd made choices for himself. And he felt overwhelmed.

One summer day he packed up his Honda Accord with a beach blanket, chair, and cooler. He drove an hour to the New England coast. At first Jacob was a bit self-conscious sitting on the beach alone. Slowly, the warmth of the sun on his bare chest and the soothing rhythm of the waves began to melt away his anxiety.

Toes buried under the sand, face flung back receiving the blessing of the salty air, he was reminded of how as a young boy he loved going to the beach with his family—building sand castles, chasing waves with his Labrador retriever, being carried to the car by his father after falling asleep under an umbrella.

On the drive home Jacob sang along loudly with the Beatles and James Taylor. Nobody cared that he sang out of tune. For the first time in months, maybe years, slivers of joy shone through like rays of life into his weary soul.

Each week during that summer of transition, Jacob would return to the beach. He took long walks along the water's edge, rode waves, and napped on the warm sand. At the end of the day he always felt soothed, calm, a little less broken. Surrounding himself in a place that he loved was a step in the direction of loving himself, others, and even God.

Practice

What Do I Love?

Start your Sabbath time with your journal, pen, and candle. Light the candle, and write at the top a page, "What do I love?" Give yourself as much time as possible to free write. Don't filter or judge. Simply write for as long as you can. What one thing on this list could you do today? When you do it, notice what you love about it. Immerse all of your senses in the activity and enjoy!

If you are taking an entire Sabbatical Day, give yourself time to savor one activity you love. Then move on to another—perhaps eating special foods, walking certain trails, painting, napping, reading, or whatever calls to your heart. Allow yourself the gift of an entire day of pursuing what you love. Ask yourself throughout the day, "What do I love?" If you begin to feel guilty, remind yourself that connecting with what you love will strengthen your connection with God, yourself, and those around you.

If you live with others, and you want them to participate, invite them along. If you need a break from others, ask for space and support. Explain that you need time to recharge your batteries. Let them know you support them in their pursuit of what they love.

DAY 29

Generous Spirit

To receive everything,
One must open one's hands
And give.

Taisen Deshimaru

After Malcolm and I got both kids settled in college, my parents took us away for a long weekend.

The morning after our arrival, someone knocked on our hotel door. A bell-hop handed Mom a "thank-you" note signed by every member of the front desk staff for a box of candy Mom and Dad had given them.

"Why did you give them candy?" I asked. "We had asked if we could have a room with a better view," Dad said. "They went to great lengths to make one available for us. We just wanted to thank them for the extra effort."

Earlier this summer, Kiki had called Mom and told her, "Grandma I'm so tired from all the end of the year busyness and college decision stuff, can I come stay with you and just hang out? I don't want to do a lot, just get away."

Mom agreed, and when Kiki arrived at their home she was assured that she had no obligation to spend time with her grandma and grandpa unless she wanted to. She could read in her room, lie out in the sun, do whatever she needed to take care of herself. As any grandparent knows, this was no small gesture. Time with grandchildren is precious indeed.

We all know people who embody a generous spirit, those of bountiful heart, who take time to consider what it is another might want and need. They give thanks for the generosity of others and they offer their gifts without expecting anything in return.

Giving with Joy

Take a few moments and remember a time when you were helping some-one, creating something, offering yourself fully; a time when you felt engaged and alive. What was the situation? What did you most enjoy about it? Give yourself a few minutes to jot down your thoughts. Then make a list of gifts you enjoy sharing, cooking perhaps, listening, or organizing. Write down whatever comes to you. Is there one gift on this list that you would like to share with another person today? Consider someone in your life that you would like to reach out to in the spirit of generosity. What might this person need or want most in this moment? Can you give freely, with no strings attached? If so, take the time to connect with the generous spirit within you and joyfully offer your gift.

DAY 30

Laughing Awake

To truly laugh, you must be able to take your pain and play with it.
Charlie Chaplin

"Remember when the kids were in kindergarten and they gave Kiki a haircut," Rhonda said, giggling, "and we were drinking wine on the back porch?" She was lying in a hospital bed, hooked up to oxygen and an IV, propped up by a pile of pillows.

"Of course I do!" I snorted as I recalled Brendan and Erin running out of the house, dragging Kiki, and proudly screaming, "Look what we did!" At the time, Rhonda and I were mortified. We had been so engrossed in our own conversation that we had lost track of the kids.

"And Kiki's pre-school picture was the next week!" Rhonda added. "Her picture was hilarious."

"Those jagged-edged bangs will forever document my incompetence as a parent!"

That afternoon in the hospital, Rhonda and I reminisced and laughed about many of our children's antics. In spite of the fact—perhaps because of the fact—that Rhonda was dying of breast cancer, we tapped into a natural well of humor to sustain us.

Laughter is good medicine. It relaxes the whole body, improves the immune system, triggers the release of endorphins (the body's "feel good" chemicals), improves the function of blood vessels, and increases blood flow to the heart. Even in the most stressful situations, laughter can provide a well-needed release of nervous energy.

Humor provides greater connection with others and promotes a feeling of well-being. Let's remember to laugh whenever we can.

PRACTICE

Laugh Out Loud

Okay, this may seem a little contrived, but stay with me on this one. Smile. Curl those lips up and crack a big old smile. That's right. I'm telling you to smile. Now relax your mouth and repeat the exercise, only smile more broadly. How does that feel? Now, let out a deep belly laugh. Don't worry that it's contrived, just laugh. If anyone at home can hear you they will wonder what you are up to. Keep them guessing. Let it fly—take a deep breath and laugh again.

When you feel you are done sit and smile for a minute. In closing, decide that you're going to find humor in your day, whether it means taking yourself less seriously, reading comics, or asking a friend, "What funny things have happened to you lately?" Consciously invite laughter into your day and enjoy its benefits

DAY 31

Preparing the Altar

An unshared life is not living. He who shares does not lessen,
but greatens his life.

Stephen S. Wise

MISS RAZ MUST HAVE SENSED my confusion. She sidled up next to me as I stared at the overflowing table of church volunteer sign-up sheets. Maybe she waited there, ready to skillfully recruit. "Hey Kid," she said. "Why don't you join me on the altar guild?" Clueless as to what this meant, but vain enough to do anything for anyone who called a middle-aged me "Kid," I scribbled my name on the sheet.

On my assigned Saturday morning, I joined Miss Raz along with Martha, Patty, and Phyllis. These experienced women patiently explained every detail involved in preparing the altar for service. Miss Raz confidently directed her troops. Martha remained close, easing my anxiety. When I forgot the name for an item she smiled and whispered, "Or you can call it the 'holy napkin.'" We refilled candelabras with oil, gently wiped them down, and presented the line-up to Miss Raz, who eyed them with drill sergeant precision. Patti and Phyllis turned piles of lilies into graceful flower arrangements.

After our tasks were complete, Miss Raz took me to the back of the nave to admire the group's work. She noticed that the candles on the altar were a bit out of alignment and went up to fix them, calling back to me, "Are they straight now?" I admired the artistry and care with which these women transformed the sanctuary.

The next morning when we arrived at church, I felt a new appreciation for all the work that goes into creating sacred space for the worship service. From the procession of the choir, through the readings, the sermon, and the guitar music during the Eucharist, I became aware of so many previously unappreciated gifts that help prepare the space and encourage our hearts to open to God and to each other.

Noticing the Gifts

Take a few moments in silence to appreciate all that went into the creation of the space where you now sit. Maybe you want to consider the people who drew the plans for the chair, couch, cushion on which you sit, and those who actually crafted it. What about the items in the room? Who gave them to you? Who worked hard to pay for them? If it was you, who gave you that work? Perhaps you want to reflect on the actual structure that is housing you and those who contributed to its coming into being. Consider the land on which you sit. Try to imagine who might have lived here hundreds of years ago.

Allow yourself to go deeply as you notice the gifts around you—who contributed to the creation, support, and care of these gifts? Remain with these images for as long as you like. Give thanks.

You may want to remember this exercise next time you go to a restaurant. Notice the amount of preparation involved—from laying out the clean silverware, to chopping ingredients and cooking food, to designing and typing the menu. As you travel through your day, carry this awareness of the abounding gifts the world offers at every turn.

DAY 32

The Wisdom of Silence

In the sweet territory of silence we touch the mystery. It's the place of reflection and contemplation, and it's the place where we can connect with the deep knowing, to the deep wisdom way.

Angeles Arrien

THE DESERT TRADITION OF THE fourth century comprised a group of Christians who felt deep concern about embracing a faith that was taking on the trappings of the Roman Empire. Many fled to the desert to maintain their unadorned contemplative Christian practices. During this time, elder women were called "Amma," and men, "Abba."

Followers were encouraged to create space for the soul to stir and to listen for the whisper of the Spirit. Silence was honored as a spiritual discipline. In her book, *The Desert Mothers: Spiritual Practices from the Women of the Wilderness*, Mary C. Earle quotes an unidentified Amma. "Silence is a way of waiting, a way of watching, and a way of listening to what is going on within and around us."

Silence offers rest—from the cacophony of radios, TVs, telephones, computers, traffic, children, any number of things. Like a spacious inhalation, silence makes room for us to breathe in LIFE.

PRACTICE

Opening to Silence

Today pick a regular activity like driving a car or cooking and perform it in silence—no radio, no TV, no telephone. You are not adding another task to your busy life; you are simply creating space around something you already do.

Listen, notice, pay attention to the silence. What is it offering you? How do you feel being in silence? Perhaps you will catch sparks of inspiration during this quiet time. Maybe nothing noticeably different will occur. Simply focus on fully experiencing the silence.

DAY 33

The Company We Keep

Through our Spirit Buddies we are loved unconditionally by the "Great Love." Our Spirit Buddies listen with warm delighted attention, witness our dreams and commitments, take us seriously, and hold us accountable for our promises.
Rabbi Shefa Gold

"Only within yourself do you know when you are really free," Sandra said, blue eyes locked on mine, willing me to understand. We were meeting at a coffee shop so she could share her experience as a member of a Wisdom Circle, a group of six women who have met for two years, intentionally supporting one another's spiritual journey.

"I couldn't live without it," she continued. "Reflecting on what the circle means to me the words 'I'm free' keep going through my head. I'm free to express my doubts, my beliefs, my disbeliefs." Delicately wrapping her long fingers around the straw of her blueberry smoothie Sandra smiled. "I know with these women I can tell the truth that is known to me now. This is important because I am not that free in other areas of my life, many things hold me back.

"Sometimes I am surprised by what I have shared and afterward I think, my goodness, is that me? But it is the deep listening which calls forth these truths. At first I was apprehensive, but trust has grown in time. Now it is like we are giving each other a holy moment that is not going to be interrupted." I nodded in agreement.

We discussed the importance of members of the group honoring the circle's guidelines to: listen devoutly without interrupting the speaker, maintain confidentiality, and speak from the heart when it is your turn. We agreed that a deep level of trust allows for speaking your truth and hearing different perspectives.

"We tell it like it is!" Sandra beamed. "And you know, I learn from other's truths."

"I love Richard Rohr's writing," she said. "He says something like, 'We are mistaken if we believe our being good matters to our Creator. What matters is that we fall in love with God. God just wants us to be in love.'" We sat silently allowing her words to linger.

"You know," Sandra concluded, "in the group we love each other. We are learning how to fall into that kind of love."

Practice

Identify Spiritual Companions

As you continue this journey of Living AWAKE, you may wish to cultivate spiritual companions to provide mutual support for growth. Let's consider this companion-building opportunity. Close your eyes and take three deep, cleansing breaths. Sit quietly and consider the following questions, one at a time:

Who in my life do I admire as spiritually awake?

Who do I see living with integrity?

If I needed to make a life-changing decision, who would I call?

Who would be excited to know that I was taking time to grow spiritually?

Write any names or thoughts that come to you in this exercise. For some of us, there may be many people who come to mind, others none. If you were able to come up with some names, consider how you might deepen your connection with them. Would you want to ask one (or more) of them to meet with you regularly so that you can support each other on your spiritual journeys?

If you do not have any names that spring forth, pay attention to this information. Perhaps you could begin noticing people who seem to live from a deep place and try to get to know them better. You could research a saint or someone from history whom you admire and look to their example when making important decisions or developing ways to live from a deeper place. Of course, this approach is secondary to developing relationships with others whom you can speak to on regular basis, but it is a start while you build connections with potential spiritual companions.

Close with a prayer, "Beloved Counselor, grant me wisdom and guidance in cultivating relationships that support my coming to know you better. May I be a loving, trustworthy companion to others. Amen."

DAY 34

Crushed by Pebbles

Wisdom comes in the mind of not knowing.
The still mind that simply is.

Stephen Levine

IMAGINE YOU WERE GIVEN AN empty bag and told to carry it with you always. Every time you chose to adopt a certainty or a "belief" that narrowed your experience of life, a small pebble would be placed in your bag. At first, carrying the bag would be a minor inconvenience, but over time, it would get heavy, hard to carry. It might even inhibit your ability to move.

Consider some of these pebbles you might have placed, over the years, in your bag:

"I have never liked exercise, and I know I never will."

"I have to have a closet filled with shoes."

"I'm too fat."

"I'll never find work I love."

"I can't forgive my parents."

We also develop beliefs about others that blind us to aspects that don't fit our story:

"If you give homeless people money they will just drink it away."

"All big businesses are corrupt."

"If you don't believe Christianity is the only true religion, I can't get along with you."

Many of us stagger along unaware that we are dragging a heavy, lumpy sack behind us, unaware that we are constantly putting limits on our lives. This is not the case for everyone though. I am inspired by a dear friend, Joe, a retired minister, who is well into his seventies. Rather than getting more rigid as he ages, Joe softens—he is open and yielding to new possibilities and different ideas. His blue eyes are light with love. Joe doesn't seem to be burdened by the weight of accumulated "stories," but rather walks through life wide open. He embraces people who are gay, straight, black, white, liberal, conservative—everyone.

In his retirement, Joe has taught himself how to publish books. If he ever told himself, "I can't publish a book," he has released that pebble from his sack. Joe is learning new things and making new friends all the time.

How do we lighten our load before our love of life gets crushed by pebbles? We could start by emptying one pebble from our heavy sack.

 PRACTICE

Removing a Pebble

Give yourself a few minutes to consider an entrenched belief. It may be a story about yourself, about others, or about how the world works. What comes to mind?

How has this "belief" impacted your life? How has it weighed you down?

Imagine removing this pebble from your sack. Take it out now. Toss it away. Consider removing another.

Perhaps by lightening our loads we will be better able to experience what life is serving up in this moment—unencumbered by a big, lumpy sack that threatens to quash our spirits.

DAY 35

Life as Art

But the pauses between the notes—ah, that is where the art resides.
Arthur Schnabel

"CREATE A BIG OLD MESS," Cathy Smith Bowers told us, her arms flailing as if she were stirring up the air. Cathy, North Carolina's Poet Laureate, was leading a poetry writing workshop at the Haden Institute's Spiritual Direction Training. The "mess" she was referring to was the writing we were to produce. "Write about an abiding image," she told us. "Do not be concerned about grammar or word choice. Just free write and make a mess."

She walked backwards, arms outstretched in a dramatic gesture. "Stand back, she said. She invited us to see what we had produced.

"Finally, chip away what is not the poem. It is important to allow both parts of the process, the creating and the chiseling."

A few days later, all of us Spiritual Direction students gathered in the intimate chapel at Kanuga Retreat Center for the graduation of the second year class. The graduates presented their final projects. Many had written papers. Someone else sewed an intricate cloth banner and another person had sculpted a statue. During the ceremony, we learned that the sculptress had been afraid she'd chipped away too much from the stone and had spoken with her mentor about this concern.

"Rarely do we remove too much," her mentor said. "In fact, usually we do not take away enough."

I have heard that an accomplished sculptor has a vision for what she wishes to create and sees the "chipping away" as a process of unearthing the inherent beauty in the stone. To craft a powerful poem, we sometimes need to delete gorgeous words and images. To sculpt a fine piece, precious stones must fall in shards on the ground.

 PRACTICE

Life as Art

Immerse yourself in a creative project. Approach this as an opportunity to connect with the Divine Creator, even if you are one of the many who does not consider yourself artistic. If any critical or judgmental voices arise, simply notice them and let them go. Give yourself permission to enjoy the process without attachment to the outcome.

Remember, this is a Sabbath day. If possible be generous with the time you offer yourself. Whatever you decide to do, **bring a prayerful, playful presence to the creative process** and invite the Divine Creator to participate. Here are a few suggestions:

- Take crayons or pencils and paper to a favorite place in nature. Sit quietly for a period of time, seeking a particular object of beauty. Perhaps it will be a small acorn on the ground, a flowering dogwood, an orange maple leaf. When you have found something that calls to you, create an expression of that object. Trace it or draw it or make a rubbing of it. Or find another way to represent it. Take time to honor the object. Let it speak to you.

- Paint something. This could be as simple as squishing your hands in finger paints and smearing swirly, nonsensical shapes, or dipping a paint brush into watercolors and covering a journal page with circles.

- If you're motivated, paint a room a soothing, fresh hue. Enjoy the opportunity to choose colors that energize you. Save colorful paint color swatches to use as bookmarks.

At the end of the day reflect on your experience. What did you learn about yourself, your life? In closing, reflect on your answers and give thanks for any new insights or ideas you have gleaned.

DAY 36

Beloved Child of God

*The Holy Spirit descended upon him in bodily form like a dove.
And a voice came from heaven, "You are my Son, the Beloved; with
you I am well pleased."*

Luke 3:22 (NRSV)

"I NEVER FEEL LIKE I have done enough. When the kids get home we have so many activities, I just run on autopilot. At work I am forever leaving a pile of unfinished business on my desk. On Sundays when I hear about all of the needs in our community, I feel guilty I'm not doing more to help out at church." Amber smoothed a strand of her blonde hair behind her ear. "How do I escape this feeling of never doing ENOUGH?"

Amber's anguish echoes the pain many of us feel. A pervasive sense of incompleteness. When we buy into the "not enough" mindset, peace is forever at bay. Our work is not good enough, our care-giving not extensive enough, our experiences not thorough enough, our lives not organized enough. Attempting to feed an insatiable hunger and forging on in the conquest of unattainable goals, we miss opportunities to celebrate the gifts of the moment.

 PRACTICE

Lectio Divina or Divine Reading

This practice is intended to be enjoyed in a quiet, peaceful environment at an unhurried pace.

Following the instructions, deliberately read the following passage out loud three times.

"The Holy Spirit descended in bodily form like a dove. And a voice came from heaven, 'You are my beloved; with you I am well pleased'" (adapted from Luke 3:22 NRSV).*

- The first time you read the passage, listen with the "ear of the heart" for a word or phrase that jumps out at you. Sit for a few minutes in silence.

- The second time, simply meditate on/contemplate what this passage may be offering you.

- After the third reading, sit in silence and allow a prayer to bubble up within you. Then, sit for a few more moments of silence before continuing on with your day.

You may wish to make notes in journal about any insights that came to you.

*Feel free to substitute a different brief passage if you like. You may want to choose text from the Bhagavad Gita, the Hebrew Bible, or another meaningful source.

Note: This is an abbreviated version of traditional Lectio Divina.

DAY 37

Gifts in the Night

*Dreams are illustrations…from the book your soul
is writing about you.*

Marsha Norman

I HAD BEEN STRUGGLING FOR months to rebuild my life. Having left a sixteen-year marriage, I was consumed by unproductive worry and obsessive planning, unsure about what steps to take.

"For so long, you have been trying to figure all of this out intellectually," my friend Susan said. "Want to look at it from a different perspective?"

"I have no idea what you're thinking," I sighed, "but I'm open to anything at this point."

"Great! One way to get out of your head and into your soul is by paying attention to your dreams. I think you might enjoy starting a dream journal."

I was excited about this unconventional approach and within days was sleeping with a notepad on my nightstand. In the morning, before my feet hit the floor, I would write down what I could recall from my dreams. Some days it seemed as if the words I wrote were unimportant. Many days I didn't have time to read my reflections. Other days a dream image stayed with me all day. After a few weeks of writing in my dream journal, a direction became clear. One morning I even wrote down the floor plan for a home that had come in a dream. A year later when I was moving into a cozy home with a wrap around porch, I realized it had an uncanny resemblance to the one I had chronicled in my dream journal.

Practice

Dream Journal

Keep a journal and a pen next to your bed.

- Before going to sleep ask for your dreams to reveal to you wisdom regarding your life. You can make this general or quite specific. Commit to write them down.

- Upon waking, immediately write down all that you can remember from the previous night. At first, it may be very little if anything at all. Most people find the more they do this exercise, the better their dream memory becomes.

  Perhaps you would like to try this for one night, one week, maybe the rest of your life.

- Over time, review your dreams and look for significant details or themes that might be helpful.

  Give thanks for the Spirit's guidance.
  Sweet Dreams!

DAY 38

Freedom from Clutter

The secret of happiness, you see, is not found in seeking more, but in developing the capacity to enjoy less.

Socrates

Our home is for sale. Anyone who has been through this process knows how emotionally and physically grueling it can be to prepare the home you live in to be toured as if it were a museum. Our real estate agent even recommended that we take most of our family photos down so prospective buyers could more easily envision their family living here. Malcolm said he feared for our agent; apparently I looked like a lioness about to leap.

Cleaning out closets, discarding items we no longer value or use, was a drudgery at first. I found myself wanting to hold on to "knick knacks" and clothes I hadn't touched in years. That old voice, "what if…" kicked in. "What if stirrup pants came back in style?"

After a couple of weekends of purging "stuff," I found my groove. Late at night I boxed up books and dragged broken down bookcases out to the garage for a trip to the dump. We carted away bags of clothing we hadn't worn in years. offering them to people who might actually wear the clothes.

I am not sure when I began to feel lighter—maybe it was the first time I dusted and there were fewer burdened surfaces. Perhaps it was the time I walked into my closet and could immediately find what I was looking for. This concentrated effort to release things we do not treasure or need has been freeing for Malcolm and me, on many levels. We also value more that which we have chosen to keep.

Jim Vucuolo, my teacher at the Institute of Life Coach Training, put it this way: "The external reflects the internal." For me, one of the residual benefits of de-cluttering is that I'm better at focusing on tasks.

This process has also affected how I shop. Now, before I buy something to bring home, I try to take a moment and consider, "Is this truly valuable to me? Will I want to clean it? Take care of it? Move it?" If the answer is no, it stays right there on the shelf. I'm not as good at stimulating the economy as

I once was, and I still have a long way to go on this simplicity journey, but I am enjoying these first steps toward freedom.

PRACTICE

Declutter

Take a few minutes and rest quietly. Enjoy the gift of silence. Ask yourself, "What is one thing that I could remove from this home?" Sit with the question and allow at least one item to come to mind. Go to that item. Recycle it, throw it out, or give it away—today. Remove another item. Pause before purchasing something new. Evaluate. Ask yourself: "Is this of value to me? Do I need it?"

Perhaps you'd like to set aside an afternoon to declutter. Reflect on how you feel after you've cleared clutter from your space.

DAY 39

Hands Wide Open

For everything there is a season, and a time for every purpose under heaven.

Ecclesiastes 3:1

Brendan draped his long arm over my shoulder. "Mom, I think it's time to say goodbye." He was right. There was nothing more to do. We had put the sheets on his bunk bed, unloaded his belongings into the dorm room, and were now standing in awkward silence. Sadness clung in the air like San Francisco fog. I stepped forward to hold him close; he loosely returned my embrace. When Malcolm, Kiki, and I reached the car, I folded into my seat. Guttural sobs flowed out of me in waves.

Two weeks later, we delivered Kiki to her freshman college dorm and attended her convocation. The chaplain approached the lectern; we all bowed our heads and prayed. Fearful thoughts gave way to remembering what I love about this school: the intimacy, the honoring of the sacred, and the commitment to make the world a better place. In only minutes, ritual provided much-needed comfort to my uneasy soul.

Perhaps in hopes of framing our personal stories in the context of The Story, the university president quoted Ecclesiastes, "For everything there is a season."

After the ceremony Kiki walked to the parking lot with us to retrieve a few final items from the car. Echoing her brother's words she said, "Mom, let's say goodbye here." We held each other close and then I opened my hands to set her free. It was her season to move on, mine and Malcolm's to channel our energy in other directions.

Kneeling in church the next morning, waiting to receive the Eucharist, I looked down at my hands. They didn't feel open; they felt empty. And yet, these same hands that had held Brendan and Kiki as babies had just released them to the world; these hands were open, ready to receive, to raise up and give thanks. I sensed that this grieving would take time; that some moments I would feel empty and others quite open. I owe it to Brendan and Kiki to honor them by trying my best to fully embrace the empty and make space for the open. I reminded myself that I would always be their mother despite the speed at which my role in their lives seemed to be diminishing.

PRACTICE

Hands Wide Open

Sit in silence for a few minutes. Place your hands palms up, resting them on your thighs. Tightly clench your fists and then release them. Repeat the exercise as many times as you like, clenching, then releasing, clenching, then releasing. Look at your hands and notice how you feel with each movement. When you are finished, remain quiet, and from the depth of the silence ask yourself:

- What am I clinging to right now?

- What am I being called to let go?

- What that is new is being created in my life?

In closing, offer a prayer of thanks and ask for wisdom and courage; invite them to guide you through all seasons of your life.

DAY 40

Living Awake

Contemplation is the highest expression of man's intellectual and spiritual life. It is that life itself fully awake, fully active, fully aware that it is alive. It is spiritual wonder. It is spontaneous awe at the sacredness of life, of being.

Thomas Merton

RECENTLY ONE OF OUR FRIENDS brought over his two young daughters. His wife was out of town and he wanted to watch a football game with Malcolm. I got to play "auntie" for a couple of hours.

It has been a while since small children have blessed this house. I took the girls into Brendan and Kiki's rooms and they picked out two huge stuffed St. Bernard dogs to play with. We laid the dogs on the carpet. I would count, "One, two, three!" and the girls would jump onto the stuffed dogs, clinging to their necks, laughing. Again and again they flung themselves onto the dogs, each jump followed by squeals of glee as if it were the first jump.

Their joy was infectious. Their ALIVENESS energized us and our entire home.

Little children remind us how to live AWAKE—with wonder and joy. They play until they're worn out and need a nap. They make funny faces. They dance, laugh, and love. They know how to look, how to SEE.

At what age do we stop seeing that we do in fact live on the funniest and most beautiful planet? When did I first drive home without noticing the setting sun and the pasture of white calves tinted pink from the brilliant colors? What would it be like if tomorrow morning, instead of "getting out of bed," I decided to "wake up"? Even if my day isn't filled with stuffed St. Bernards to jump on; even if it feels like there are a few Rottweilers nipping at my heels, I wonder if my experience of life wouldn't be richer if I engaged all of my senses in this process of being—eyes and heart fully open. I hope I will be inspired by the girls to LIVE AWAKE.

NOTICE

Sit quietly and NOTICE what you think, hear, smell, taste, see, and touch. Engage all of your senses. Stay with this heightened awareness for at least ten minutes. What colors are you drawn to? What emotions are you feeling? What thoughts arise? Perhaps you want to stay with one image for the entire time, like watching a breeze blowing through trees. Or maybe you prefer to observe as many different things and sensations as possible. No judgment. No right or wrong. Just NOTICE.

When you are finished, make a commitment to yourself. Tell yourself to bring this kind of NOTICING to your life every day.

Staying Connected

Congratulations! You did it. You held true to the promise you made to yourself forty days ago. Certainly this is cause for celebration. I hope you will find a way to honor yourself and enjoy your accomplishment. If you feel finished, wonderful! There is no need to read further. If you are wondering, Where do I go from here? I have a few suggestions.

Perhaps you want to reflect on how taking this time impacted you. What surprised you? What seemed easy? Difficult? Give yourself the gift of acknowledging and assimilating what you have learned in these forty days.

Continue to devote fifteen minutes or more to re-connect with yourself and the Beloved. Like any relationship, this one will flourish under the nourishment of your attention. One of the most powerful aspects of the program you just completed was the discipline of showing up each day. There is no need to stop.

Over the last forty days you have been introduced to a number of prayer and reflective practices. Perhaps you wish you'd had more time with some of the exercises. If so, go back and linger over those for as many days as you like.

Maybe you'd like to choose a practice or combination of practices, like Centering Prayer or journaling, to try regularly.

If you would like to have a partner to walk with you on the journey, find a companion to support you as you continue to live from a deeper, more AWAKE place. Invite a friend to go through the forty-day program with you, create a Living AWAKE Circle (See Resource section for details), or seek out a spiritual director.

Finally, Resources (p. 167) offers books, websites, and other material to assist you in living AWAKE. Use them as you see fit. You have planted many seeds these past six weeks. Now you can water them. NOTICE what catches your soul's attention and feed your soul every day.

Thank you for journeying with me. I am honored. You, my fellow traveler, have been in my heart and prayers throughout the process of creating this book. My ongoing hope and prayer is that you will continue to find ways to feed your soul and remember that you are a beloved child of God.

Namaste,
Mary Bea Sullivan

RESOURCES

INTERESTED IN SHARING THIS EXPERIENCE with a small group? Perhaps you would like to create a Living AWAKE circle. **Download a free Facilitator's Guide at www.marybeasullivan.com.** This is an ideal tool for book clubs, faith groups, anyone interested in traveling this 40-day journey in community rather than alone. Weekly exercises and facilitation tips make forming a group easy.

You will also find information about Mary Bea Sullivan's work as a spiritual companion, inspirational speaker, and facilitator at this website. Contact Mary at mary@marybeasullivan.com for speaking, facilitation, or spiritual companionship availability.

Below are additional resources you might find helpful.

WEBSITES

www.cacradicalgrace.org	Fr. Richard Rohr
www.carolhenderson.com	Writing Coach/Editor
www.contemplativeoutreach.org	Centering Prayer
www.hadeninstitute.com	Spiritual Direction/
	Dream Leader Training
www.deanalanjones.com	Dean Alan Jones
www.kagyu.org	Lama Norlha Rinpoche

Resources

www.marybeasullivan.com · Retreats/Blog/ Facilitator's Guide/ Spiritual Companion

www.project-compassion.org · End-of-Life Care

www.sdiworld.org · Spiritual Directors International

BOOKS

Bourgeault, Cynthia, *Centering Prayer and Inner Awakening*

Bourgeault, Cynthia, *Mystical Hope*

Bourgeault, Cynthia, *The Wisdom Jesus*

Bozarth, Alla Renee, *Life is Goodbye/Life is Hello: Grieving Well Through All Kinds of Loss*

Earle, Mary C., *The Desert Mothers: Spiritual Practices from the Women of the Wilderness*

Jones, Alan, *Soul Making: The Desert Way of Spirituality*

Keating, Thomas, *Open Mind, Open Heart*

Lindbergh, Anne Morrow, *Gift from the Sea*

McGehee, Mary, OSB, *My Heart Rejoices*

Merrill, Nan, *Psalms for Praying*

Merton, Thomas, *Care of the Soul*

Mitchell, Stephen, *Bhagavad Gita*

Mitchell, Stephen, *Tao Te Ching*

Muller, Wayne, *How Then, Shall We Live?*

Muller, Wayne, *Sabbath: Finding Rest, Renewal and Delight in Our Busy Lives*

Nouwen, Henri, *Spiritual Direction: Wisdom for the Long Walk of Faith*

Remen, Rachel Naomi, *My Grandfather's Blessings*

Sullivan, Mary Bea, *Dancing Naked Under the Moon Uncovering the Wisdom Within*

Tiwari, Maya, *Ayurveda: A Life of Balance*

Whitworth, Laura, *Co-Active Coaching*

ACKNOWLEDGMENTS

THIS BOOK WAS A COLLABORATIVE effort. I am grateful to my editor and friend, Carol Henderson, for her guidance and skills throughout the project. Carol is gifted at "walking beside" in a way that encourages and challenges. She has helped me to find the writer within and for that, and her sense of humor, I am profoundly grateful.

As I mentioned in the introduction, the genesis for this book came from my blog, www.marybeasullivan.com/blog. A number of readers encouraged me to make this available to a wider audience. Thank you to Elizabeth Downs, Jane Hull, Caroline Humphries, Margaret Krohn, Sandra Lawler, Sarah Shelton, and Angie Wright for providing the enthusiasm which fueled the beginning of this work.

Three pilot groups read the manuscript and completed the exercises. Their feedback was invaluable and the book is much better because of it. Thank you to Lane Tutt and the Lenten Circle at Nativity Episcopal Church, Huntsville, Alabama, and Ann Caretti, Frances Charles, Tracy Clancy, Diane David, Betty Denton, Kelly Ross-Davis, Jeanne Jackson, Kati Smith, Debi Swaney, and Kathy Thomson. The spirit of your experiences are infused in these pages.

Living AWAKE includes stories from family and friends. Thanks to all, especially Jenny Nolen and Ruth Deramus for sharing your experiences in the hopes of helping others. It is not always easy to be the child of a writer who draws from her own life. By default, Brendan and Kiki have generously shared their stories. I am grateful for their good humor and support.

Acknowledgments

There were times along this journey when I questioned the value of the project. During these times, encouragement from Bob Blackwell, Ellen Dossett, Ina Durham, Joe Elmore, Stephanie Gamon, Kathleen Christa Murphy, and Mary Whetsell was especially valuable. We all need our cheerleaders—I am fortunate to have these friends on my team.

Most of all I want to thank my beloved husband, Malcolm. Never in my wildest dreams could I have imagined a better life partner and best friend. I am so fortunate to have him in my life. In addition to being loving and fun, Malcolm inspires me to try to be the woman he sees.

PERMISSIONS

FORGIVENESS PRAYER ON DAY 25 from Alla Renée Bozarth, from *Life is Goodbye/Life is Hello: Grieving Well through All Kinds of Loss,* Hazelden 1982, revised edition 1988; *Dance for Me When I Die,* audiocassette, Wisdom House 1986; *A Journey Through Grief,* Hazelden 1990; *Love's Prism: Threads of Grace Through Seasons of Change,* Sheed and Ward/Rowman and Littlefield 1995; and *This Mortal Marriage: Poems of Love, Lament and Praise,* iUniverse 2003.

Centering Prayer on Day 11 and Welcoming Prayer on Day 16 from Contemplative Outreach, Ltd., 10 Park Place, 2nd Floor, Suite B, Butler, NJ 07405. 973-838-3384. www.contemplativeoutreach.org

LaVergne, TN USA
09 November 2010
204041LV00003B/4/P